Indigenous Evangelists Contributions Towards Zeliang Baptist Churches in Nagaland

Indigenous Evangelists Contributions Towards Zeliang Baptist Churches in Nagaland

Ideuraibe Putlang

Christian World Imprints

First Published in 2021 by

Christian World Imprints
Christian Publishing & Books from India
C-3, Wazirpur Industrial Area
Delhi-110052
cwidelhi2017@gmail.com
www.ChristianWorldImprints.com
Phone: +91 11 41526079

ISBN: 978-93-5148-505-6

Printed in India.

Dedicated to all the
Pioneer Evangelists
of ZBCC

That the book in its original form is the thesis submitted to the Senate of Serampore College (University), towards the Master of Theology (M.Th.) degree and is published with written permission. The candidate is responsible for the title, contents and opinions expressed in it.

The original title of the thesis is, *The Works of Local Evangelists towards the Growth of Zeme Naga Baptist Churches.* But for the purpose of publication with due acknowledgement and the permission required, the title of the Thesis is reconstructed to the present form.

Contents

Foreword-I

It is a privilege for me to write the Foreword to the book *Indigenous Evangelists Contributions towards Zeliang Baptist Churches in Nagaland* by Ideuraibe Putlang. He is a young upcoming Historian. He studied his Masters in the department of History of Christianity at Eastern Theological College and successfully completed his M.Th in first class.

The present book is an outcome of his sincere research for his M.Th thesis. He has touched upon a very important topic which has been neglected or forgotten by many. In every region, the Native Evangelists have played a tremendous role in the origin and growth of Christianity. Unfortunately, often this aspect of history has not been given due recognition and credit. In the present research, Mr. Ideuraibe meticulously studied the role of the native Evangelists among his community – the Zeliang Nagas of Nagaland. This was done through countless personal interviews with persons who knew or had connection with the Native Evangelists. Hence, a pioneering work hitherto unknown has been accomplished through this research.

This should serve as primary sources for their History of Christianity. It is indeed a well-researched study with proper documentation. Further, I hope this will serve as incentive for further research to be done by younger generations to come.

The book has four chapters; the first presents the historical background of the Zeliang Nagas, their general background, socio-cultural, economic, political and religious life along with the Heraka belief system. Chapter two presents a very detailed analysis on the advent of Christianity and the growth of the churches, beginning with the first missionary contact till the dissemination of the associations. The third chapter vividly narrates the life sketch of the four significant evangelists namely Keneise Meru, Heizieding Kediteiheing Lungalang, Hazieding Hairangbuing and Wisungbo Nrak. The final chapter is an intriguing discourse on the works and contributions of the evangelists.

It is my belief that this well-researched book will act as a good resource for scholars and also a good read for anyone interested in learning about the redeeming history of the Zeliang Nagas. May this book touch the hearts of the readers to remember the goodness of God and be inspired to contribute more towards the ministry.

Rev. Dr. Prof. Narola Imchen
Principal
Eastern Theological College, Jorhat

Foreword-II

Prior to the celebration of the centenary of Christianity in Zeliang areas, beautiful churches had been planted in almost every Zeliang villages. We are happy and proud of the rapid growth of Christianity and progress of the Zeliang Churches. Regret to say that today, many failed to acknowledge and give due credit especially to the local evangelists who tirelessly pioneered in the growth of Christianity and church planting. Generally, we tend to give credit to the Western Christian missionaries but in fact, the Western Christian missionaries did not set their foot in the soil of the Zeliang Naga. In every field pioneers faced many challenges and problems and that was true to the pioneers of Zeliang Christians.

I appreciate Mr. Ideuraibe Putlang for venturing this area and wrote in his research entitled: *Indigenous Evangelists Contributions towards the Growth of Zeliang Baptist Churches in Nagaland* which is very important but often neglected. In this book the writer attempted "to re-discover the pioneering works of the native evangelists" who had contributed for the growth of Christianity and the growth of Zeliang Naga Baptist churches. He also delineated the contributions of the early converts or the local zealous evangelists namely, Rev. Keneise Meru, Rev. H. K. Lungalang, Rev. Hazieding Hairangbuing and Evan. Wisungbo Nrak towards the growth of Christianity and church growth/planting bearing all pains and selfless sacrifices which were often side-lined.

Reading this book will unearth many things which you have never heard of the pioneers. I am sure that this book can be a helpful tool for the upcoming researchers especially in the field of the growth of Christianity and Baptist churches in Zeliang Naga as well as the preachers and believers alike. I believe that this book will enrich our knowledge and have a great impact in our life with the sacrificial acts of the pioneers. It is my wish and prayer that many young church leaders will make a good use of it for the glory of God. And I congratulate Mr. Ideuraibe Putlang for the effort invested to come up with this book. I wish the writer and the book a great success.

Mr. Izieteilung Terieng
Executive Secretary
Zeme Baptist Church Council, Nagaland

Preface

The trajectory of spiritual and social life is eminently with the anecdote of Christian history. Therefore, it is important to know one's own history in this modern progressing world. The focal point of this book is to explore the works and sacrifices of Zeliang native evangelists collectively, whose contributions have abolished some diabolical systems practiced in the past and had established a new generation. An attempt has also been made to highlight the background of the origin and migration narratives of the Zeliang people, who are settled in the three states of Assam, Manipur and Nagaland since the era of British rule. This book is a recollection of memories of collective native Christian pioneers whose works and hope for the people to whom they ministered with the Gospel, will be the course of spiritual and social life of the people.

The credibility of the gospel is often regarded with highest esteem and is placed on the highest altar. As such scores of scholars in the region assert and affirm gospel as the main source of transformation in the society. The dawn of the gospel in the region had ushered in radical transformation which benefitted not only individuals but also all the stake holders involved. Similarly, the beginning of 20th century shifted the Zeliang society in a better way, when the colonial British Empire and western Christian missionaries set their foot in the soil of the then Naga Hills. The efforts of the western missionaries have led to some significant awareness among the people who have encountered the missionaries and in return they carried forward the legacy of the missionaries to a great extent. But, many a time the contributions of these pioneers or the early converts were often neglected due to the failure of the native Christians to maintain records unlike the western missionaries. Likewise, as one penetrates through the series of monologues related to the history of Zeliang Christians, rhetorical presentation of the growth was visible yet the contributions of the local evangelist were side-lined. No doubt the credit goes to the western missionaries. However, rapid growth of Christianity was experienced only after foreign missionaries left. Thus, the research work attempted to re-discover the pioneering works of the native evangelists who have equally contributed for the growth of Christianity.

The early converts who have embraced Christ did not let their faith go wasted. Just like the "white man's burden," the early Zeliang evangelists with the blessings and responsibilities endowed and empowered on them journeyed forth to convince their people to embrace Christ and His teachings. In this journey, many of their people obnoxiously turned them down but anxiously with undeterred determination and farsighted vision they could contribute immensely for the society at large. Besides their vocations of spreading the gospel and church planting, they could also contribute towards establishing Christian education centre and literature ministry. It is also to be noted that there are many other pioneers who have indisputably contributed equally from the first generation of Christianity among this people. Thus, the magnanimous works of these evangelists manifested a new society with an enlightened mind and a faith deeply rooted in Christ. Hence, basing on this fact the research has attempted to bring out the life and contributions of the selected four pioneers namely, Rev. Keneise, Rev. H. K. Lungalang, Rev. Hazieding, Evan. Wisungbo, whose contributions ought not only recognition but should be imprinted and written for the remarkable impacts they have brought crossing all human boundaries through their zealous and selfless sacrifices. The contribution of other contemporary evangelist like Rev. Turi, the first ordained minister among the Liangmai, who have worked with these pioneers evangelising the whole Zeliang area.

Nheubuing, Lunzie, Deuhing, Huzubo, Bikau and others are beyond doubt, remarkable. They have equally shouldered the responsibility to the contribution of the growth of the churches apart from the selected four evangelists, but the research is limited only to the four evangelists with an aim to provide their biographical account and their contributions.

Ideuraibe Putlang

Acknowledgement

This book, *Indigenous Evangelists Contributions towards Zeliang Baptist Churches in Nagaland,* is based on my thesis which I have submitted to Senate of Serampore College (University) in partial fulfilment of the requirements for the Degree of Master of Theology.

I would like to thank the following for their contributions and support during my study and writing of this research.

Almighty God for His unceasing love and guidance. For giving me wisdom and good health all throughout my studies and helping me to accomplish this research work. I cannot adequately express thanks enough to Him for several outstanding individuals whose help are indispensible in the production of this research.

My deepest thanks and gratitude to Rev. Dr. Narola Imchen, Professor of History of Christianity and Principal, Eastern Theological College, Jorhat, for writing the foreword. Her valuable guidance, genuine encouragement and skilled direction throughout my research work, enabled me to complete my research.

My gratitude to Mr. Izieteilung Terieng, Executive Secretary, ZBCC, for writing the foreword for my book.

I also wholeheartedly thank Rev. Dr. Elungkiebe Zeliang, Associate Prof. of History of Christianity and HoD, Conflict Management and Peace, Martin Luther Christian University,

Shillong, who helped me design this work and making me available the essential materials.

I also acknowledge the generous help and efficient guidance of Rev. Dr. Woba James, President of CHAI-North East India, President of Peace Rider, India, Member of Board of Studies (History of Christianity), Senate of Serampore College, Associate Prof. of History of Christianity, ETC, Jorhat.

Heartfelt thanks and appreciation to Mr. Epetlung Lungalang, and Dr. Rampaukopoing for reading through the manuscript, giving valuable suggestions and encouragement till the accomplishment of this publication.

I am also grateful to Mr. Zailung Thou, Ms. Iteibeule, Ms. Idolule Putlang, for the positive support in contributing profoundly towards the completion of this research.

I am indebted to my family members for their continuous support all throughout my life. My entire relatives, friends and my church members who stand by my side and assisted me, helping and moulding me thus far in my theological studies.

Ideuraibe Putlang

Abbreviations

ABFMS	-	American Baptist Foreign Missionary Society
BET	-	Basic Education Training
CBCAM	-	Council of Baptist Churches in Assam and Manipur
FGN	-	Federal Government of Nagaland
GOI	-	Government of India
IMS	-	Impur Mission School
ISC	-	Intermediate of Science Course
JMS	-	Jorhat Mission School
KFCC	-	Kohima Field Church Council
KMF	-	Kohima Mission Field/Kohima Field
KMTS	-	Kohima Mission Training School
LBA	-	Liangmai Baptist Association
MTSK	-	Mission Training School, Kohima
NBCC	-	Nagaland Baptist Church Council
NEI	-	North East India
NNC	-	Naga National Council
ZBA	-	Zeliang Baptist Association
ZBA	-	Zeliangrong Baptist Association
ZBCC	-	Zeme Baptist Church Council
ZCNEI	-	Zeme Council of North East India
ZKA	-	Zeliang-Kuki Association

General Introduction

1. Statement of the Problem

The proposed research work intends to investigate the role of local evangelists in spreading Christianity leading to the expansion of Zeliang Baptist churches in Nagaland.

2. Elaboration of the Problem

The Zeliang Nagas are one of the major tribes of North East India. They lived in a compact and contiguous geographical area comprising of the Tamenglong district and a part of Senapati district of Manipur, the Peren district and a part of Dimapur of Nagaland and the Halflong sub-division of North Cachar Hills district of Assam.[1] The Zeliang Nagas lived an independent, self-sufficient and contended life till the advent of the British rule in the 19th century.

Christianity came to Zeliang area at the close of the 19th century. The spread of Christianity in the Naga Hills was hastened by the group-effort of the foreign missionaries and the establishment of British Government in north east India. Though their zeal to spread the Gospel reached out to many parts of the states, no foreign missionary came and established church in this land. While

1 Makulim Remei, *Zeliangrong Union: The 71st Commemoration of Zeliangrong Solidarity Day* (Imphal: HopCom Offset Printers, 2005), 2.

applauding with tribute to the western missionaries for their epochal works done, Christianity was spread to Zeliang churches through the work of native evangelists. The Gospel of Christianity was first brought to them by the Angami evangelists. The contribution of these native evangelists from neighbouring tribe was a noble and notable one as it impacted towards this local people. It is to be reminded that it geared the initiation of evangelism when the first Zeliang got converted to the gospel of Christ. The first Zeliang to be converted to Christianity was Mr. Heizieluing of Benreu village in 1897,[2] which also became the first village to have church among the Zeliangrong villages.[3] In 1905, the second church was established in Mpung (now Tampung) village through the conversion of Irangteing.[4] However, the growth of Christianity was not rapid as the American Baptist Mission could not penetrate much in some areas, due to the presence of the British Government in the Naga Hills. Nevertheless, it was not so discouraging, the little seed that they have sowed was carried forward by the local evangelists. Evangelists such as Rev. Keneise Meru, Rev. H. K. Lungalang, Rev. Hazieding Hairangbuing, Evan. Wisungbo Nrak and many other pioneers who are not mentioned here have carried forward the legacy of spreading the gospel and contributed to the growth of the churches among the Zeliang Nagas.

The evangelists played a very significant role in spreading the Gospel to the people. Keneise Meru, prior to his ordination was the pillar of the early Zeliang Christians. He worked actively in evangelizing the whole area and nurtured the early converts, even reaching out to the non-Christians. In 1939, he was ordained by J. E. Tanquist and became the first ordained minister of the association. H. K. Lungalang had to resign from the government job and sacrificed his life for his people, since there was no capable leader then to lead the association. In May 1951, he was appointed as the first Field Director (Executive Secretary) of the Zeliang-Kuki Association.

2 *Benreu Baptist Church Centenary (1997) Souvenir* (Benreu: BBCC Committee, 1997), 17.

3 Elungkiebe Zeliang, *Charismatic Movements in the Baptist Churches in North East India: A Zeliangrong Perspective* (Delhi: ISCPK, 2014), 40.

4 *Mpung Baptist Church Diamond Jubilee Souvenir* (Mpung: Souvenir Committee, 1988), 3. Cf. E. Zeliang, *Charismatic Movements*, 40.

Thereafter, his contribution in many capacities in the expansion of the church, mission, education, literature was laudable.[5] Extensive evangelism done by Hazieding along with his other pioneer team accelerated the growth of Christianity in the whole area. Wisungbo, the first convert from Tening Village, although he was partially blind, after his baptism in 1927, became very active evangelist in the area and through his effort several churches were born during the early days of Christianity in the Liangmai area of Nagaland.

The growth of Baptist churches was very slow because of bad communication and confrontation of traditional faith. However, these evangelists worked to meet the need of the people in and around the area in spreading the gospel and evangelizing the people. In such manner, in spite of strong opposition from the followers of traditional religion and *Heraka,*[6] Christianity had its preponderance to many villages. Yet, the contributions of these local evangelists are merely accepted and have not been given sufficient attention in spite of their important works. No adequate recognition of their involvement has been given in writing and their contribution is at the verge of being forgotten. Therefore, the researcher intends to document and account the important contributions of the local evangelists particularly the four above mentioned evangelists. No doubt, there are also other evangelists who have equally contributed to the growth of the churches among the Zeliangs. But, the research is limited only to the four evangelists keeping in mind the limitation of space and time of this research.

---

5 E. Zeliang, *Charismatic Movements*, 41.

6 *Heraka* is a belief system which is very common in North East India and is found only among the Zeliangrong community. Heraka religious belief system was believed to be revealed through Haipou Jadonang and Rani Gaidinliu in 1920s by *Tingwang*. It is monotheistic in belief that there is omnipotent omnipresent god, who is the root cause of all creation, the creator of the universe who is all in all. *Heraka* means pure, with no assimilation of evil things. The word *Hera*-refers to God and *Ka*-meaning, fence. It means God separating the evil gods and kept his people inside his fencing. Those who are kept inside the fencing are called *Herakame*, which means, the pure people. *Cf.* Ramkuiwangbe Newme, *Tingwang Hingde* (Guwahati: Regional Zeliangrong Heraka Association, Assam, 1991), 1.

3. Importance of the Research

The research is important mainly for three reasons:

1. Firstly, an adequate chronicles of the beginning of Christianity among the Zeliang Nagas is still lacking. This research is a modest attempt to fill that gap.
2. Secondly, the contributions of the local evangelists have not been brought to ample attention so far, for which a significant appreciation is necessary.
3. Thirdly, this study will brought to the fore the importance of the roles the local evangelists played during the formative years of the Zeliang churches.

4. Scope and Limitation of the Study

This research will be limited to the Zeliang Nagas, focusing on the Christian pioneers in Nagaland as an important account of church history among the Zeliangs. However, to support its research, it will also include the general history of Zeliangrong Baptist Association.

5. Previous Research

The unpublished literature of the earlier research work with regard to the history of Christianity has been done like, "The Impact of Christianity on Social and Religious Life of the Zeliang Nagas" by H. Hiakie, (BD Thesis, 1989). "A Historical Study of Christianity and Heraka (*Kampai*) Cult among Zeliangrong People in Nagaland" by Haisuitei, (BD Thesis 1989). "The Impact of Christian Gospel on the Traditional Superstitious Beliefs of the Zeliangrong Nagas," by Haiku, (BD Thesis, 1995).

Few published literature that has long description about the story of Christianity are like "The Zeliangrong Nagas: A Study of Tribal Christianity" by Ramkhun Pamei (1996), "Zeliang Nagame Na Tingwang Sam" by Visor H. Zeliang (1982) and "History of Zeliangrong Baptist Churches in Nagaland: 1897-1993" by Rabi Pame (2015). However, there is no specific written record done by any researcher on the role and contribution of pioneer evangelists, though some writings in the forms of reports and records have been done. So far no research has been done on this topic. Therefore the researcher will make an in-depth study on the growth and expansion of the Churches through the works of local pioneers.

6. Method and Source of the Study

This research is a historical analytical method to examine and acknowledge the native evangelists using vital people resources, empirical study like interview and questionnaires. It will also employ relevant and resourceful written documents.

7. Hypothesis of the Study

1. No proper acknowledgement towards the growth of churches and mission work done by pioneer evangelists among the Zeliang churches.
2. It assumes that it is important to note that Zeliang churches' history is incomplete without remembering its pioneers.

8. Structure of the Research

The research is divided into four chapters. In order to give a comprehensive overview of the research focus, the first chapter introduces the general historical background of the Zeliang Nagas, the land, culture and tradition of the people.

The second chapter discusses the advent of Christianity in the area and the growth of the churches.

The third chapter is the biographical study, introducing their early ministry, their wives, and their main works, leading to the contribution and the expansion of the churches.

The fourth chapter deals with the works of the Four Evangelists, which is also the main focus of the research. It discusses and analyses their works and contributions as pioneers of the church growth.

Finally, the study brings to a close with an evaluation and general conclusion.

1

Historical Background of the Zeme Nagas

Introduction

The Zeme[7] inhabits in a geographically contiguous area but are politically divided into three states such as Assam, Manipur and Nagaland. The land of the Zemes includes the present Peren district

---

7 Since the time of Britishers, for the sake of administrative conveniences these people have been kept under the different administrative units calling them with different nomenclatures-the *Zeme, Liangmai, Rongmei*. The *Zeme* and *Liangmai* are designated as *Kacha Nagas* and *Rongmei* is known as *Kabui Nagas,* as they are named by the foreigners. However, the composite name Ze+Liang+Rong is used rather than *Kacha* or *Kabui* Nagas or the like which was given by outsiders. Here the writer intends to explore the Zeme Nagas of Nagaland but it will use 'Zeliangrong' inclusively whenever needed to convey both to the Rongmei, Liangmai and particularly to the Zeme as the research is intended to be. N. Saha, "Ethnographic Study of the Zeliangrong Tribe of North East India," in *The Tribes of Northeast India,* edited by Sabastian Karotemprel (Calcutta: Firma KLM Private Limited, 1984), 218. *Cf.* M. P. Namthiurei, *The Great Awakening* (Manipur: Tamenglong GJ Publication, 1972), 7; B. B. Kumar, *Naga Identity* (New Delhi: Concept Publishing Company, 2005), 23.

of Nagaland, part of Tamenlong district and part of Senapati district in Manipur, and part of Dima-Hasao (Halflong) district of Assam. This people are an ancient community of North East India who have been in occupation of these three states. The Zeme people have various oral traditions regarding their origin and migration. They are tribals from the Mongoloid stock and their physical features are by and large similar to the other tribes of North East India. Historically, the Zeme, Liangmai and Rongmei have regarded themselves as single ethno cultural entity with their common legends of origin and their ancestral migration, though they are now scattered to different regions. However, this study focuses on the Zeme Nagas and its historical background to which the research is connected.

1. Geographical Background in General

The Zeme country covers a compact and contiguous area namely Tamenglong District, Western Sadar Hills, Loktak Project area of Manipur State, the Halflong Subdivision of North Cachar Hills District of Assam and the Peren district of Nagaland State.[8]

The Zeme people have been inhabiting their present homeland covering a compact and contiguous area from Barail Range and its Southern branches, from the Dhansiri Valley in the North, including the present Churachandpur District of Manipur in the South, the Bhuban Hills and the Jiri River and the Halflong plateau in the West adjoining the Angami, the Mao-Maram Hills in the north-east.[9] The land was divided and kept under three different administrative units by the British-Indian Government in the early parts of the 20th Century for their administrative conveniences. As a result of this trisection of Zeliangrong country into three states-Nagaland, Manipur and Assam, it resulted in much inconvenience and great disadvantages for the people.[10] This complex history of the Zeliang territory was the fragmentation of the people and their lands into different administrative units by the more powerful conquerors.

8 Gangmumei Kamei, *The History of Zeliangrong Nagas: From Makhel to Rani Gaidinliu* (Delhi: Spectrum Publications, 2004), 2.

9 Saha, "Ethnographic Study of the Zeliangrong Tribe," 218.

10 Rabi Pame, *History of Zeliangrong Baptist Church in Nagaland 1897-1993* (Nagaland: Nzauna Baptist Church, 2015), 5.

Thus, the geographical fragmentation of their ethnic territory is a cruel historical legacy which the Zeliangrong people have been trying to undo for the integration of the entire land under one umbrella in modern times.

2. Zeme

Zemes are one of the Zeliangrong kindred tribes. The name, *Zeme* was derived from their settlement at the hill range, which was the frontier of the Zeliangrong habitat as *Zena* or *Nzie.* From this the people were known as *Zeme* or *Nzieme.*[11] The etymology of the word *Zeme* has different meanings and interpretations. In the 19th century writer like J. H. Hutton apply the word *kacha,* by which he meant Zeme.[12] However the word *kacha,* is said to have derived from the word of Angami Naga as *ketse* or *ketsü,* which is translated as deep forest or dweller of the forest.[13] Whatever the term *Zeme* is supposedly interpreted, the word *Zeme in* Zeme dialect is *Zena, Nzieme,* or *Zemena* means, *man* or *the people,*[14] who lived in the slope area or valley.[15]

2.1. Identity of the Zeme Naga

The Zeliangrongs now inhabiting in Nagaland are mostly Zeme. They are one of the three kindred tribes of Zeliangrong Nagas, as the name Zeliangrong is an acronym of three families; Zeme, Liangmai and Rongmei. The first syllables of each of these names *Ze+Liang+Rong* are the combination of Zeliangrong.[16] Due to historical misconception and colonial confusion, the Zeme and Liangmai in Manipur state are officially designated as *Kacha Naga*

---

11 Kamei, *The History of Zeliangrong Nagas,* 36.

12 J. H. Hutton, *The Angami Nagas* (London: Macmillan and Co. Ltd., 1921), 352.

13 Kamei, *The History of Zeliangrong Nagas,* 13.

14 Namthiubuiyang Pamei, *The Trail of Makuilongdi: The Continuing Saga of the Zeliangrong People* (Tamenglong: Gironta Charitable Foundation, 2001), 19.

15 A. Nshoga, *Traditional Naga Village System and its Transformation* (Delhi: Anshah Publishing House, 2009), 41.

16 Kamei, *The History of Zeliangrong Nagas,* 10.

and Rongmei as *Kabui Naga.* However in North Cachar Hills of Assam, the name *Zeme Naga* is used officially. In Nagaland, Zeme and Liangmai are known as Zeliangs.[17] They occupy the south-west fringe of Nagaland with a land endowed with the third highest mountain of the state called Mt. Pauna and the most envied state reserved forest called Intangki Forest. The Zeme has two geographical features-hill ranges on the east and extensive plains on the west marked by the Dhansiri river in Assam.[18]

2.2. Origin and Migration

As P. D. Stracey, an admirer of the Naga culture and tradition has remarked, "the biggest mystery is the origin of the various tribes of Nagaland,"[19] as the origin of the Nagas remain a protracted debate because the history was passed on through oral account. However, it is commonly understood and taken for granted that the Naga family all over the North East were from one stock of race migrated in waves either from China or Vietnam through Burma[20] and the origin of the Zeme was always stressed on Makhel and from Makhel they moved down in search of land for settlement in Makuilongdi. Thus, the ancestral home of the Zeliangrong is Makuilongdi, a village situated in present Senapati district of Manipur. There is a tradition that says the number of houses inhabited by the Zeliangrong in Makuilongdi reached 7777 which demanded for a migration to new places. So the Ze, Liang, and Rong started to migrate and spread to the present Nagaland, Manipur and North Cachar Hills of Assam that pushed down their settlement as far as Churachandpur district of Manipur and beyond Halflong.[21]

Tracing the oral traditions of their origin and migration which clearly tells about their settlements, it points to several historical places like *Makuilongdi, Nruire-Kikie* and *Kajinglong* of their migration.

---

17 Pame, *History of Zeliangrong Baptist Church in Nagaland,* 11.

18 Suitei, "Zeme Baptist Church Council (ZBCC)," in *From Darkness to Light,* edited by Alongla P. Aier (Kohima: NBCC, 1997), 90.

19 P. D. Stacey, *Nagaland Nightmare* (New Delhi: Allied Publishers, 1968), 9.

20 Pamei, *The Zeliangrong Nagas,* 24.

21 Pamei, *The Zeliangrong Nagas,* 20.

While *Makuilongdi* served as the main centre of the migration of the Zemes,[22] *Nruire-Kikie* was the sub-centre of the Zemes. Their traditions agree that they are the descendants of the three sons of Nguibabe,[23] *the Chief of Makuilongdi.*[24] These three sons lived together in *Makuilongdi* for years as their father was the chief of the village where one of the sons of chief Nguibabe was *Namhegang*, who is the ancestor of present Zemes.[25] Thus, *Makuilongdi* was the cradle of Zeme culture.[26] The Zeme people are mongoloid in appearance, mostly with thick black hair, well built and their eyes with epicanthic folds. They are quite, gentle and friendly. Linguistically they belong to Sino-Tibetan group.[27]

2.3. Zeme of Nagaland

The Zemes were descended from Nguibabe's (chief of *Makuilongdi*) eldest son, Namhegang (Namgong) who after his failure to succeed his father, left his parents and went out to establish a new village name *Hereira*, which is regarded as the first village.[28] The Zemes in search of land moved out in mass from the central region of *Makuilongdi* and crossed the Barak River. From the banks of the river they moved in directions of their choices. Some of the groups proceeded towards the north range of Peren and sustained their northward expansion where they encountered the Angamis into the present northern Zeme country.[29] Today, the Zeme occupy the Jalukie Valley, Bakie valley

---

22 Pamei, *The Trail of Makuilongdi,* 19.

23 According to the traditions, the three sons of Nguibabe were the ancestors of the *Zeme, Liangmai* and *Romgmei* respectively. Nguibabe's eldest son was Namhegang (ancestor of Zeme), Nrimbangbe (ancestor of Liangmai) and Keding (ancestor of Rongmai and Inpui). Zeliang, *Charismatic Movements,* 6-8.

24 Nshoga, *Traditional Naga Village System,* 39.

25 Pamei, *The Zeliangrong Nagas,* 19.

26 E. Zeliang, *Charismatic Movements,* 6.

27 Sipra Sen, *Tribes of Nagaland* (Delhi: Mittal Publications, 1987), 43.

28 Kamei, *The History of Zeliangrong Nagas,* 36.

29 Pamei, *The Trail of Makuilongdi*, 20.

and the surrounding hills of the Nagaland state. They are called the northern Zeme people.[30]

The Zeme of Nagaland confines mostly within Peren district that borders to Kohima in the north, Dimapur in the northwest, Assam southwest and Manipur on the east. Thus, Peren district is dominantly inhabited by the Zeme villages, though there are also several villages of Liangmais and Kukis under Tening sub-division.[31] As per the Zeme Council of North East India, 2012, altogether there are 79 villages of Zeme Nagas of Nagaland.[32]

3. Socio-Cultural Life of the Zeme

Every society, whether primitive or civilized has its own way of living, conduct, administration, codes and manners. It is so with the Zeme Nagas. They had their own way of living and the most social aspect of the Zeme is the communitarian ways of life and cultural customs.

3.1. Family

The family is the smallest unit in a village. Generally the type of family is simple, consists of husband, wife and children. The term family in Zeme is *kelak* which is derived from *kelakteibe,* meaning marriage. When a man marries and set up a house of his own, his house is called *kelaki.*[33] It is a social ideal of the Zeme that parents lived together with their married children for some time. When the married couple establishes new house of their own after a year or more, they stay separated from their parents and only the youngest son live with the parents. However, separation caused by marriage does not hamper the family ties and the love of his or her parents.

There is no doubt that in traditional Zeme society, the family is the basic social institution. Parents and children's love respect each other and the parents expect their children's support and care in their

30 Pamei, *The Trail of Makuilongdi*, 20.

31 Raitu Elu, Haisoyi Ndang & N. H. Pouheu, comps., *Zeme Council North East India: Zeme Cultural Heritage & Customary Laws* (N.p.: Zeme Council North East India, 2012), 10.

32 Elu, *Zeme Council North East India,* 10.

33 Interview with Paukwet Hengame, Deacon, New Tesen Baptist Church, 5 May 2016.

old age. Adhering to patriarchal social system, the head of the family had more responsibilities for their domestic harmony. Teknonymy, a custom of avoiding calling a person name directly is commonly practiced. This is obligatory in traditional Zeme society.[34]

3.2. Custom of Marriage

In relation to marriage, Zeme practices exogamy outside of family or clan. On no account may a man marry a woman from his own clan. Bachelors and young men marry the young women and girls of another clan. Exogamous marriage was encouraged on biological reason and inter-clan marriage was encouraged with a belief that the relationship and understanding among the clans are improved in the society.

According to Pame, the marriage among the Zeme is classified into four types. Two of which are considered as ordinary marriages and the other two are counted to be honourable and prestigious marriages.[35] The first type of marriage is a marriage of young widow or woman who has already had a child illegally. This marriage is conducted in a very simple way and bride price is usually not involved in this ordinary marriage. The second type of marriage is by means of elopement and seducement to which the couple make their union before marriage is solemnised. The society condemned and despised such type of marriage. The third is the type of marriage which is arranged through proper channel of negotiation. This is a valid marriage arranged between a man and a woman and is performed in accordance with the existing traditional customs. This marriage is greatly honoured and accepted by the Zeme society which has been practiced from time immemorial as their tradition. The fourth type of marriage is a holy marriage, which is the highest degree and the most respectful and honourable practice of marriage in Zeme custom.[36]

---

34 Rabi Pame, *Culture and the Church: History of Zeme Naga Baptist Church NC Hills, Assam 1910-1995* (Nagaland: Nzauna Baptist Church, 2015), 24.

35 Pame, *Culture and the Church*, 26. *Cf. A Brief Account of the Zeliangrong Nagas* (Guwahati: All Zeliangrong Students' Union-AZSU, AMN, 2009), 35.

36 Pame, *Culture and the Church*, 27.

Marriage is one of the most important occasions in the life of men and women and is proudly honoured. Generally both the young men and women are encouraged to marry when they attain maturity. Young people are free to choose their own life partner.[37] T. C. Hudson said, "Many marriages are arranged by the young people themselves on the basis of affection."[38] This does not mean they ignore their parents' consent. Certain rules are given to those who are willing to get married, such as marriage within the same clan is forbidden by the law of exogamy at the same time marriage outside the village or tribe was not encouraged in the traditional society.[39] The bond of marriage is considered permanent unless it is separated by death or certain unavoidable divorce.

3.3. Boys' and Girls' Morung/Dormitory

The morungs were the centre of Naga social life. It was a place where young people were trained. It is also the most and finest ornate buildings found in Naga villages with its unique nature as the most outstanding aspect of the social life.[40] The most characteristic feature of Zeme life is the prevalence of morung system which is a social institution and the life vein of cultural activities. At least two or more will be found in the village according to the size and population of the village. In Zeme dialect the boys' morung is known as *Rehangki* and *Releiki* for girls. The members of the *Rehangki* are collectively known as *Kiangna* while those of *Releiki* are known as *Kileuna.*[41]

Any kind of tribal education and discipline- the art of warfare, handicraft, music, and dance, moral and social education are taught in the morung. They organise dance and social work for the whole village.[42] Thus R. R. Shimray rightly called "the morungs and the

37 Pame, *History of Zeliangrong Baptist Church in Nagaland,* 23.

38 T. C. Hudson, *The Naga Tribes of Manipur* (Imphal: J. M. Printing Works, 1994), 87.

39 K. S. Singh, ed., *People of India: Nagaland,* vol. XXIV (Calcutta: Seagull Books, 1994), 174.

40 P. T. Phillip, *The Growth of Baptist Churches in Nagaland* (Guwahati: Christian Literature Centre, 1972), 33.

41 Pame, *Culture and the Church,* 28.

42 Pamei, *The Zeliangrong Nagas,* 30.

lady's dormitories are the Naga Schools."[43] It is the core of village institution, through which the moral values, art of life, and material culture etc. are derived. The morung is like a synagogue for the Zeme but these types of dormitories are fast disappearing in almost all the Zeme villages due to the invasion of the modern pattern of life.[44]

3.4. Status of Women and Elders in the Society

There is no class distinction in the Zeme society but because of the patriarchal system women do not enjoy the same status as the men with respect to public activities, council affairs, right to have the paternal property and the male occupational heavy works.[45] Yet, the Zeme women played a major role in productive economy and household management. They were not appointed to a priestly office in the village, kept under man's domination, their daily wages differed, but are expected to be an equal partner in agriculture and home building.[46] They participated in every field both in domestic and outside work which in some way worked more than men.

Elderly people are also highly respected in Zeme community life. When an old man enters a morung, all the boys will stand up and give enough space for the elders to sit and after that only younger ones sit. No one dares to joke or call an elders name. Old people are highly respected and are well taken care of and most of the things will be done with their consent.[47]

3.5. Festivals

As a whole, Nagaland is a land of festivals and ceremonies. The festivals of the different tribes are similar to each other with the exception of its name and method of celebration. The Zeme people observe and celebrate festivals which are connected to the occupation

---

43 R. R. Shimray, *Origin and Culture of Nagas* (New Delhi: Samsok Publications, 1985), 193.

44 Interview with Hainsu Kauring, Church elder, New Tesen Baptist Church, 19 December 2016.

45 Saha, "Ethnographic Study of the Zeliangrong Tribe," 220.

46 Pame, *History of Zeliangrog Baptist Church in Nagaland,* 25.

47 Pame, *History of Zeliangrog Baptist Church in Nagaland,* 25.

of agriculture. Each festival is marked with spiritual sentiments, evoking the blessing of *Tingwang* for protection of crops or at the other festival, thanksgiving for the bountiful harvest and so on.[48] Among many festivals, *Meleingi* is the most important festival.[49] *Meleingi* is celebrated to herald spring for a rigorous, prosperous and healthy life for all human being and is held in Spring marking the start of the sowing seeds.[50]

Festivals are interlinked with spiritual sentiments and the predominant themes of all the festivals are offering of prayers to the Supreme Being. Nevertheless, it is also related to seasons or stages of agriculture operation.[51] Festivals are joyful occasions for everyone and it is marked by people adorned in festive dress with different colours which expresses the joy and fun felt by all. Various dances are also performed during this time.[52]

3.6. Folk Dances and Tales

Zeme are also fond of dances and songs. They are particularly known for their art of dance. Commenting on their dance B. B. Ghosh remarked;

> The Zeliangrong people are very good dancers and their women also dance together with men. Of all the dances of the Nagas, the dance of the Zeliangrong is the best.[53]

Dances are accompanied by songs and musical instruments like drums and cymbals (gongs). There are different dances in which men and women dance together and sometimes separately. In a war dance, men with splendid physics and rippling muscles hold spears

---

48 Elu, *Zeme Council North East India,* 82-83.

49 Sen, *Tribes of Nagaland,* 46.

50 Pame, *History of Zeliangrong Baptist Church in Nagaland,* 26.

51 Prakash Singh, *India- The Land and People: Nagaland* (New Delhi: National Book Trust, 1972), 69.

52 Pame, *History of Zeliangrong Baptist Church in Nagaland,* 26.

53 B. B. Ghosh, *History of Nagaland* (New Delhi: S. Chand & Company Ltd, 1982), 260. *Cf. A Peep into a Rich Naga Culture* (Kohima: Directorate of Information and Public Relations, 1987), 47.

and javelins with shields to enact a battle making terrifying howls, shout and war whoops. Dances such as these are mainly performed during festivals.[54]

The Zeme also have many folktales and folklores. Some of the tales are love stories like *Herie, Senting,* humourous tales like, *Asa-Maiserung, Asampei, Ceube and Heradi,* and tales of orphans like *Heriegongna, Nkiemsong.*[55] Besides, there are many folksongs that either accompanied the folktales or sing alone as separate songs.[56]

4. Economic Life of the Zeme

In the traditional Zeme society, the wealth of a man was determined by the land he possessed, the quantity of paddy available in the granary, number of domestic animals, ornaments and money. Although a small section of the population of Zemes are now engaging in non-agricultural occupations like government service, private business, etc. Almost all the Zemes economy is based on agriculture by tradition though it is primitive because they depended on land, water, forest as the main economic resources.

4.1. Land

Land is considered as the best wealth among immovable property of the individual or village. It held a vast area of forest under its protection. This holding system of land has three types, individual, clan and village land in which all the products and taxes go to the owner of the land.

A village reserved forest is usually maintained near the village, to protect against fire incident, random felling of trees and encroachment of its land which falls under this forest. Forest is also one of the major assets. It was one of the most important resources of the village economy. Many of the youth used to ply with forest

---

54 Pame, *History of Zeliangrong Baptist Church in Nagaland,* 28.

55 Some of the Zeliangrong folktales are now compiled and translated into English. Kangzangding Thou, *Roots: A Collection of Zeliang Folktales* (Dimapur: Heritage Publishing House, 2008).

56 E. Zeliang, *Charismatic Movements,* 12.

products and earn their livelihood with variety of timbers from the forest.[57]

4.2. Agriculture

Majority of the Zemes are agriculturists. Agriculture based on jhum cultivation is the primary cultivation of the people. They adopted the jhum system of cultivation but terrace cultivation is also practiced by some of them in suitable sites. Every village has their own plot of land in the larger unit and in the smaller unit every clan and family has their own land and fields for cultivation. Every family produced enough food for their own needs from their land and lived economically self sufficient.[58] Begging is also practically nil among the Zemes.[59]

Food crops like rice, maize, millet, pulse, chilli, potato, tomato, pumpkin, ginger, brinjal, squash, cucumber etc., and also fruits like mango, guava, papaya, orange, plums, banana, peach and berries are also available. Besides these, domestic animals like cow, pig, chicken, buffalo etc., were also reared.

4.3. Trade and Barter System

Traditionally, the Zemes do trade and business system through their indigenous tools and implements and exchanged with each other. Sometimes instead of exchanging their tools, the needy people will labour in the field of the owner for the needed tools for a day or two depends on the cost of the tools.[60] In those days barter system was also practiced because of the lack of money. It was a system of exchanging goods without involvement of money for the needed goods. In this barter system all sorts of vegetables, food and other indigenous product of items that are cultivated in the farms or made of hands are also bartered.[61]

---

57 Nshoga, *Traditional Naga Village System,* 105.

58 E. Zeliang, *Charismatic Movements,* 12.

59 Pamei, *The Zeliangrong Nagas,* 26.

60 Elu, *Zeme Council North East India,* 81.

61 Pamei, *The Zeliangrong Nagas,* 25.

5. Political Life of the Zeme

The common sense of identity in Zeme society has been political organisation. In the pre-colonial days, political institution of the Zeme people is the village, which was free from outside control and is independent in every aspect of their own political affairs.

5.1. The Role of Village Chief

Before the coming of the British and their new system of government, Zeme had no tribal political organisation and their polity was village based. Many villages have heredity chiefs called *hegwang.* A village chief played multiple roles which include convening and presiding the village council which the elders from different khels and sometimes every male in the village attended.[62] Thus, E. Zeliang stated that Gangmumei Kamei has rightly observed the Zeme political form of the village as "gerontocracy with a democratic ethos is the nature of the Zeme polity."[63]

5.2. Village Polity

According to the Nagaland Regulation (Transitional Provision) each village have got a village council and each tribe a tribal council,[64] so also is with the Zeme Nagas. The village is an independent state and acts as a unit in all things. As Shimray rightly quoted, "Whether or not the village is always a social, political and religious unit. The fact remain that it was an independent unit ... the village is an independent unit in tribe."[65] The people of the village are bound together by social, political and religious ties. J. P. Mills also rightly stated that, "with all Nagas the real political unit of the tribe is the village."[66]

The village gives protection and security to individuals. The Zeme village government system is purely democratic which is governed by the village council. However there is usually a chief

62 E. Zeliang, *Charismatic Movements*, 14.

63 E. Zeliang, *Charismatic Movements*, 14.

64 Sen, *Tribes of Nagaland*, 15.

65 Shimray, *Origin and Culture of Nagas*, 14.

66 J. P. Mills, *The Aos Nagas* (London: Oxford University Press, 1973), 176.

or headman, gaon-bura, village chairman who is vested with some authority to officiate at village activities. In most cases the chief hold the leadership followed by the representatives of various clans or adult members in the village.[67] The village council is responsible for settling all the disputes, theft, adultery which is decided in accordance with their customary laws and order of the village. The village council of the elders is now called the Panchayat.[68]

6. Religious Life of the Zeme

The Zeme traditional religion is also basically similar to the type of religion found among other tribes of the Nagas. Phenomenally, the Zeme are God fearing people. Their strict observances of all kinds of rituals, gennas, taboos, and ceremonies related to their belief depict their strong sense of fearing god. They believed that there are many gods - *Hera* and spirits - *Herui,* who are responsible for the welfare of the people.[69] However, there is one omnipotent universal God called *Tingwang,* who is the Supreme Being and beside that there are many deities of benevolent and malevolent who control evil and virtues of men's life, that come to some extend of animism in their belief.[70]

6.1. Belief in Supreme Being

The Zeme religion was originally partially animism and partially theism because both polytheistic and monotheistic elements were found in their beliefs.[71] The Zeme conceived in their beliefs that there are many gods-*hera,* but the Supreme Being is *Tingwang,* king of the substantial and celestial world, who is the creator of heaven, earth and universe. He is the sustainer of all living and inanimate objects both in the terrestrial and celestial realms.[72]

Though there is no definite hypothesis or theological formulated theory attributed to Supreme Being, the Zeme people

67 Pame, *Culture and the Church,* 40.

68 Sen, *Tribes of Nagaland,* 16.

69 Saha, "Ethnographic Study of the Zeliangrong Tribe," 221.

70 Elu, *Zeme Council North East India,* 114.

71 Pame, *History of Zeliangrong Baptist Church in Nagaland,* 15.

72 Pame, *History of Zeliangrong Baptist Church in Nagaland,* 15.

called and conceived with different names like *Heratingrangpui, Tingwang, Ngaukemakrampau.* These names refer to the same Being and are interchangeably used. They believed that it has supernatural power which moves everything and is not limited to this earthly prosperity but goes beyond the life after. He is above all gods, goddesses and spirits and is known to all men.[73]

6.2. Belief in Spirits

Besides the Supreme Being, the Zeme generally believed to have two types of spirits-benevolent and malevolent spirits. There are also number of gods, goddesses and spirits whom the Zeme believed to be involved in different activities. The spirits are thought to have their abode in steep rocky places, dense forests, streams, banks of rivers, ruined old villages and uninhabited places.[74] These spirits have their separate assigned abodes in distinct places and exercise their power within their limitations.[75] These deities were worshipped because of fear and offerings were made to appease them. The benevolent spirits were the helpers and healers of men and the malevolent spirits were the evil spirits, ghosts, the life eater and afflicters of men.[76]

6.3. Concepts of Life after Death

The Naga concept of the life after death vary from tribe to tribe but there is a general understanding that the soul does not perish at death.[77] The Zeme believe in the existence of soul after death where the soul is believed to go to the land of death called *Heruiram.* The condition of life after death will be determined by the kind of life

73 Izieteilung Nsarangbe, "The Belief in the Supreme Being from the Zeliangrong Nagas Perspective: Tribal Christian Theology," in *Tribal Christian Theology: Methods and Sources for Constructing a Relevant Theology for the Indigenous People of North East India,* edited by Razosiele Lasetso and Yangkahao Vashum (Jorhat: ETC Coordination Program, 2007), 279.

74 Pame, *Culture and the Church,* 82.

75 Pamei, *The Zeliangrong Nagas,* 35.

76 Nsarangbe, *The Belief in the Supreme Being from the Zeliangrong,* 291.

77 Najekhu Yeptomi, "Early History of the Nagas," in *From Darkness to Light,* edited by Alongla P. Aier (Nagaland: NBCC, 1997), 17.

he lived on earth.[78] The actual final departure of the soul from the living happen only when the purgatory rites are performed on the particular day called *Hekak.* This ritual *Hekak* is observed at the end of the year to bid farewell and wish a favourable life in the new world.[79]

It is believed that when a person dies, things and properties which belonged to them are buried together for their next life in *Heruiram.* Failing to include their essential materials would perhaps cause the deceased to disturb the family in a rasping voice. So, this custom is strictly adhered because of the fear of poltergeist.[80] The ancestor worship was not practiced among the Zeme but there is a belief that their soul did not go too far during the first week or more also. So they offered rice, curry and rice beer to the death soul.[81]

7. Heraka[82]

Heraka is a socio-religious movement of the whole Zeliangrong Nagas started by Haipou Jadonang,[83] for the preservation of its indigenous religion and culture. *Heraka,* literally means 'pure' in Zeme, and it is a reformed religion believed to be revealed through Haipou Jadonang and Rani Gaidinliu[84] in 1920s by *Tingwang.* It believes in the supreme God, *Tingwang,* the creator of everything, and does not believe in the worship of spirits or smaller deities. It is monotheistic in belief that there is omnipotent omnipresent god, who is the root cause of all creation, the creator of the universe who

78 Pamei, *The Zeliangrong Nagas,* 35.

79 Pame, *History of Zeliangrong Baptist Church in Nagaland,* 21.

80 Pame, *History of Zeliangrong Baptist Church in Nagaland,* 15.

81 Pamei, *The Zeliangrong Nagas,* 36.

82 See footnote 7 for more detail.

83 Haipou Jadonang was born in 1905 in the village of Kambiron, Manipur. He was figured as the freedom fighter of the Nagas.

84 Rani Gaidinliu was born at Luangkao village in the Tamenglong district of Manipur 1915. She was portrayed as the freedom fighter by Jawaharlal Nehru who fought against the British, a prophetess by her followers, and an anti-Christian by the Christians.

is all in all.[85] It is a revitalised form of belief from the traditional religion with an established worship place with a synthesis of monotheistic belief, Hindu idolatry and temple worship practices. It is a simplified religious movement to revive the common origin of the political integration of the Zeliangrong people revolting for independence, identifying with the greater national struggle for India's independence alienating against the British rule for self-governance.[86]

7.1. Belief System

The mode of practice in *Heraka* religion is performed through both devotional and sacrificial with an aim to bring good and prosperous life to all men by *Tingwang*. Observing sacrificial sunrise prayer during every full moon day is strictly observed, where the young and old enjoy the animal sacrificial meat with ritual precepts to made oneself clean and powerful on this day. They have their established worship place called *Kelumki* to congregate on rituals and others related to their belief. This service is presided by *Paipei* and *Paipui*, called holy men and women who live near the *Kelumki*. They have their bible consist of the fundamental rules and hymnal book. The virtue of good and prosperous life to individual and collective through the grace of god, relation between god and evil, do and don't with reward and suffering, and their god, the supreme god is also visualised.[87]

Today, despite its strong belief system, many adherents of *Heraka* religion are converted and had embraced the faith of Christianity. However, there are still a good number who follow and practices this religion as a traditional value of their faith. Thus, it is demanding to the people of Zeme with the responsibility to work

85 Pautanzan Newmai, *The Basic Facts of Heraka Religion: Preceptress of Heraka Religion* (Imphal: Zeliangrong Heraka Association, NEI, 1993), 4.

86 Elu, *Zeme Council North East India,* 119. Cf. Gangmumei Kamei, *Jadonang: A Mystic Naga Rebel* (Imphal: 2009), 96.

87 Interview with Haireiwangbe Zeliang, Evangelist, NC Hills, 11 October 2014.

selflessly among the non believers to convert them wherever they present.[88]

Conclusion

In this chapter it describes the historical background of the Zeme Nagas. It is learnt that the socio-economic political and the religious life of the Zemes are splendid and independent until the advent of Christianity. There are various customs and habits which have valuable elements in it that makes this people unique and particular. The rich cultural heritage remains an immemorial treasure in the life and thinking of the people till today. It is an important task to put into written record rather than just embedded into passing memory of the people of these annihilated cultures. On the other hand, the primitive society which has existed for many centuries among the Zeme people had been stagnant in culture and economic life, less political impact and socially backward when we compare to the modern society. This conceivably is due to the lack of progress in the belief system, in scientific discoveries and knowledge as they embedded so much to the traditional way of life and remained isolated from its existence without exposing much to outside world.

88 Interview with Lungchi, Ex-pastor, Old Tesen Baptist Church, 21 September 2015.

2

Advent of Christianity and the Growth of the Churches

Introduction

Until the advent of the British administration in Nagaland, the pre-Christian Zeme society was for many years living a life of isolation unaware of the advantage of being exposed to outside world. They hardly had any outside contact or were influenced by other culture. However, with the establishment of British government in Kohima, the isolation of the Zeme people was exposed and explored. They were forced to come to Kohima occasionally under the administration of the Britishers to meet the demands of the British rulers. On the other hand, as the spread of Christianity among the Nagas began with the coming of American missionaries like Miles Bronson, E. W. Clark and others in the 1830s, the seed of Christianity was sown and germinated and finally it spread to all parts of Nagaland. Thus, Christianity reached the Zeme Naga through the Kohima Mission Field under the works of local evangelists from Kohima.

1. First Missionary Contact of the Nagas

The story of Christianity among the Nagas began with an American Baptist Missionary. The first village that came in contact with the gospel was Namsang village in Tirap District of Arunachal Pradesh in 1839, by Miles Bronson. However, the introduction of missionary work became more prolific through the initiation of E. W. Clark in 1872, when Clark sent his evangelist from Assam, one of his converts by the name Godhula Rutus Brown[89] to Naga Hills, particularly in Ao area.[90] It is considered that the years 1872-1955 was the period of foreign missionary era in the Naga soil. The work of evangelism began to grow in Nagaland when the American Baptist missionaries started working in the Naga Hills from 1872. The missionaries supervised the works in the Hills from Assam. Although the early missionaries faced much opposition and resistance in the course of their work, they continued to do mission which eventually led to the widespread of Christianity among the Nagas. Facing an initial opposition the gospel began to gain ground and ripple across the hill tribes. Among the Nagas, the Aos were the first to be contacted with the missionaries in their own homeland in 1872 when Clark and Godhula Brown, an Assamese convert, entered into the Naga Hills.[91] Clark coming to this area paved the first foundation of church and the further beginning of Christianity in the soil of Naga Hills.[92] Godhula also played an equal role as that of the foreign missionaries in the history of Christianity in Nagaland. He was an Assamese convert,

89 Godhula was the eldest son of Kolibar, a Sibsagar washer-man. He had his primary education from Orphan School at Nowgong, Assam. It is said that he used to disturb the missionaries but later he changed his mind and converted to Christianity. He was appointed as teacher in Sibsagar Mission School where Clark learnt Assamese from him. Joseph Puthenpurakal, *Baptist Mission in Nagaland: A Historical Study and Ecumenical Perspectives* (Shillong: Vendrame Mission Institution, 1984), 63.

90 B. B. Ghosh, ed., *Nagaland District Gazetteers: Mokokchung District* (Kohima: Government of Nagaland, 1979), 58.

91 Renthy Keitzar, ed., *Triumph of Faith in Nagaland* (Kohima: NBCC Office, 1987), 2.

92 Pathenpurakal, *Baptist Mission in Nagaland,* 80.

native evangelist of India who ventured with the gospel to his neighbouring state of Naga Hills with his wife Lucy along with Clark and open up to the spread of Christianity.

2. First Zeme Contact of the Gospel

2.1. Kohima Mission Field

With the appointment of Charles DeWitt (CD) King to Kohima by the Home Board of American Baptist Foreign Missionary Society (ABFMS) in 1878, the Kohima Mission Field was established in 1879. During the early years of Christianity with the foreign missionaries, all the Christians within Kohima Elekha (district) were grouped together as "Kohima Field" and this Field covered several tribes like: Angami, Chakesang, Zeliang, Kuki, Rengma, Mao, Poumai and Southern Sumi tribes.[93] The first convert under the Kohima Field was Sieliezhu Angami. He was baptised on 21st June, 1885. However, for eighteen years there was no record of conversion among the Zeme since the beginning of mission in Kohima.[94] It was only in1897, with the baptism of Heizieluing, the first church was established in Benreu village. Thus, the story of Christianity began among the Zeme with the first baptism of Heizieluing. This was followed by the second church in Tampung village in 1907.[95] But in the real sense the growth of the church was still very slow and there was no real progress of the church.

2.2. The Growth of Christianity

At the close of 19th century, while Christianity is seen as new religion in many parts of the world, the Zeme had in contact with Christianity from the Angami convert. No foreign missionary came

93 F. S. Downs, *The Mighty Works of God: A Brief History of the Council of Baptist Churches in North East India,* 2nd ed. (Guwahati: Christian Literature Centre, 2014), 117. *Cf.* Zhabu Terhuja, "Angami Baptist Council of Churches (ABCC)," in *From Darkness to Light,* edited by Alongla P. Aier (Kohima: NBCC, 1997), 57.

94 Phillip, *The Growth of Baptist Church in Nagaland,* 80. *Cf. Zeliangrong Baptist Association Nagaland Silver Jubilee-1954-1979* (Peren: ZBAN Silver Jubilee Souvenir Committee, 1979), 8.

95 E. Zeliang, *Charismatic Movements,* 40.

and established church to this land, although the seed of the gospel was sown by the American missionaries to the Nagas. The Gospel was first brought to them by Angami Evangelists since the Zeliang tribe were also under the Kohima Mission Field.[96] The Zeme traces their origin of Christianity through the conversion and baptism of Heizieluing in 1897. Heizieluing Meru, son of Heluikieswang of Benreu village in Nagaland was first converted by Angami evangelist named Nieser of Khonoma village and baptized by an American missionary Sidney White Rivenburg at Impur in 1897.[97] The Kohima Mission Training School Annual Report of 1906 states that three students were baptized on December 31, 1905; one of them was Kacha Naga, a former name used for Zeliang.[98] As early as 1904, Heizieluing after his conversion established a little house of worship and worked among his own people, evangelising to people who are still holding on to their traditional faith. The 92nd Annual Report of S. W. Rivenburg in ABFMS 1906 states, "the headman of one of the Kacha Naga villages is now working as an evangelist, having learned to read the scriptures."[99] This report is accounted to Heizieluing, during which in his initial years in the missionary work, he could convert many people from his village. In 1905, Iriedaung and Heirielung were converted and in 1912 six more people were baptised by Rivenburg from the same village. In 1914, Heluikieswang, Heizieluing's father and Ileuteile were baptised at Kohima during the Third Kohima Christian Association at Neherma. These early converts were the products of Heizieluing who served as evangelist until his death in 1918.[100]

The second person to be recorded by name was Irangteing, son of Hereukiang from Mpung village who was baptised in 1898 at

96 Visor H. Zeliang, *Zeliang Nagame Na Tinggwang Sam: The Zeliang Nagas and the Word of God* (Shillong: Rita Printers, 1982), 9.

97 *Benreu Baptist Church Diamond Jubilee Reha 1981* (Benreu: BBCDJ Committee, 1981), 11. *Cf.* Visor H. Zeliang, *The Naga Baptist Family* (Kohima: Council of Naga Baptist Churches, 1988), 10.

98 Quoted in Phillip, *The Growth of Baptist Church in Nagaland*, 124.

99 Quoted in *Benreu Baptist Church Centenary (1997) Souvenir* (Benreu: BBCC Committee, 1997), 24.

100 *Benreu Baptist Church Diamond,* 8-9.

Khonoma Baptist Church.[101] After his conversion he faced so much of persecution and trials from the non-Christians. The villagers were so angry with his conversion and condemned him for breaking the religion of their ancestors. Because of his conversion, the village then declared that no Christian would be permitted within the land. Amidst this opposition, he continued to be strong and courageous to overcome and later he was joined by five members to believe in Christ. However, the antagonism continued and at last Christians were driven out from the village.[102] Despite, the opposition from non-Christians and other faiths, with the baptism of Heizieluing from Benreu village, the gospel spread to the Zeme area in Nagaland. These few early converts slowly spread Christianity in Zeme area. They worked wholeheartedly and spread Christian faith to every village though it was a steady progress.

2.2.1. Native Evangelists from Kohima District

The early Zeme Christians were less and weak because of the lack of trained Christian workers. Therefore, the factual historical background of the early Christians of Zeme people would be bias without mentioning the native evangelists who came helping and associated with the infant churches in their formation period, especially during 1901-1954.

It is learnt that after the first baptism of Zeme, the Angami Christians from their established church visited this area very often to keep and nurture the new believers. Nesier Angami of Khonoma village was credited as the key person who evangelised almost all the Zeme villages and shared the gospel and baptised many people in the area. Ngulphu one of the earliest evangelists during the Zeliang-Kuki Baptist Association had baptised many Zeliang Christians. Sozang, Pekho and Sapthang served the churches in various levels.[103] The visit of Kalicharan, Ketholelhou, Khrietsovi

---

101 *Mpung Baptist Church Diamond*, 3. *Cf.* Zeliang, *Charismatic Movements*, 40.

102 "Irangteing," in *One New Humanity in Christ: Nagaland Baptist Church Council celebrates Platinum Jubilee 1937-2012* (Kohima: Documentation and Publication Committee, NBCC, 2012), 132.

103 Pame, *History of Zeliangrong Baptist Church in Nagaland*, 45.

in Tesen village and served as pastors and teachers.[104] The ministry of women was initiated by women like Visietono and Thenumezhu who went to Poilwa village and shared the gospel of God's love and educated the children which are also recorded.[105] Many others who helped and associated with different Zeme churches for further extension of his Kingdom also have their name recorded.[106] Without the help and guidance of the native evangelists from the neighbouring tribes, the church in this area would have been something other than the present one. As far as the expansion of Christianity in the early period is concern, their noble deeds in general are remembered even if their names and deeds in particular have gone unnoticed or forgotten in the passage of time.

2.2.2. Foreign Missionaries who Visited the Zeme Area

The foreign missionaries were neither stationed in Zeme area, nor did they establish their mission and church. However, they visited the Zeme Christians from time to time with the burden to encourage them and to ensure that proper footing was established in the area where the gospel could be reached to all the villages in Zeliang land.[107]

Between 1901 and 1954, foreign missionaries paid a visit to this area. Their works and visitations are worth mentioning through whom the steady growth of Christian population in this area are hastened. The first Zeme Christian as mentioned earlier was baptised by Rivenburg from Impur in 1897. He also visited Benreu, the first Christian village among the Zeliangrong through whom more

---

104 *Tesen Baptist Church Platinum Jubilee (2003) Souvenir* (Tesen: TBCPJ Committee, 2003), 12.

105 *Poilwa Baptist Church Golden Jubilee 1938-1988 Souvenir* (Poilwa: PBCGJ Souvenir Committee, 1988), 6.

106 Evangelists mostly from Kohima namely, Kruneizhu of Kohima village, Vizekho, Kekhulhou, Sielezhu, Krusieto, Zhapuzhulie, Koulievi, Pfenuo Tholeu Khate, Khohie from Khonoma village were recorded in Benreu Centenary Souvenir. *Benreu Baptist Church Centenary,* 26. *Cf.* Pame, *History of Zeliangrong Baptist Church in Nagaland,* 45.

107 H. K. Lungalang, *Kohima Field Baptist Centenary Jubilee Souvenir* (Dimapur: Ashoka Printing Press, 1985), 42-44.

people were baptised. Missionaries from Kohima Field like A. B. Dickson, George William Supplee, Salender and J. E. Tanquist, B. I. Anderson and R. F. Delano also visited the Zeme people occasionally and professed the gospel.[108] J. E. Tanquist with the assistance of some Zeme prepared a *Hymn Book in Kacha Naga* which was to be the first hymn book ever produced in their dialect. It is also not to be forgotten that he and his friends ordained Keneise, the son of Heizieluing Meru in January 1939 at Benreu village.[109] Howard Houston also visited the area during the Zeliang Kuki Association in 1953 in which he said that he took two days to return back to Kohima.[110] Many missionaries did not lose touch of the assignment for which they were sent, ministering in and around this area, which in many ways cannot tell a story without acknowledging them. They regularly visited to ensure that the gospel is properly sown to reach to all the villages.

2.3. Early Church Life

The growth of the church was never rapid and progressive because the response to the gospel was minimal in the initial period. There was no other organised Christian congregation except the two earliest villages which the gospel has first reached. But, in spite of the little and insignificant Christian community in the midst of majority non-Christians, the chief beauty of the church life begins through the earliest converts. Not long after their conversion, they had their own house of worship which had existed even prior to 1899. When Rivenburg physically visited Benreu, the first Christian village by a trip of six days during the early part of 1901, he was much pleased to see the believers meeting up regularly. He said;

> Only about six weeks of the missionary's time were spent on this field. During this period the bungalow was dethatched and a trip of six days was made to Benreu.

108 *Benreu Baptist Church Centenary,* 26.

109 *Benreu Baptist Church Diamond,* 10.

110 Howard and Harriet Houston, *Nagaland Adventure, 1947-1953* (Dimapur: Published by L. M. Murry, 1987), 18.

> I was much pleased to find the Christians here holding regular meetings in their little chapel, although not one can read. They can talk and sing and pray. I baptised two more believers there.[111]

As persistent as in witnessing and approaching others with their faith, the early Christian community continued to grow in fellowship that by 1913 a crystal existence of an institutional and organised church was recorded in the report of J. E Tanquist. After he arrived at Kohima on January 18, 1913, he reported that;

> Aside from six Kohima district groups of Christians have their own meeting houses and regular services. All of these except one area considered part of the Kohima church, the Kacha Nagas being one of these groups.[112]

As evinced in the reports, the regular worship among the people existed although the local church in the Zeme area was not established in more than two villages. Until the establishment of Tening Baptist Church in 1926, there was no record of new church in the Zeme area other than the two established churches in Benreu and Mpung, excluding the Kuki churches in the Zeliang area.

However limited and few the churches were the early Christians embraced the gospel with solemnity. These two churches was zealous even though it was small the seed was sown in the fertile soil and gradually a faithful life of the church was started proportionately with the strong believers. Their faith was proven by their deeds. One such instance was the life and contribution of Irialung, a committed believer who generously donated a plot of his terrace field for the construction of church. He also lived a pietistic life by isolating himself to forest for prayer and fasting and was often noted for his song that he sang after he returned from the forest.

---

111 *Benreu Baptist Church Centenary*, 23.

112 J. E. Tanquist, "Report of J. E. Tanquist," in *Assam Baptist Missionary Conference of the American Baptist Foreign Mission Society: Report Part II of the Thirteenth Session held in Golaghat, January 9-18, 1915*, 31.

Zeme	**English**
Aine I yiluda	Behold! I have overcome
Herakesiabe Nimpiluda	Triumphed over the evil
Nai I caide	Though I die today
Kelungta teilung gumzielie	I will inherit eternal life
Tet ah caili gwang dilo[113]	Let Satan get behind me

The life and contribution of Kutalakpe of Mpung village also characterized the commitment and conviction of the early Christians. He made a remarkable contribution to the treasury of the church by donating handsome amount of money, conch shell and bead necklace, a buffalo and a goat in the early days of Christianity. The examples set by the early converts reflected their faith towards the stability of the churches from the material and financial dependency.[114] This was one of the landmark periods for the church as the intensive support of local people saw their earnestness towards the church.

2.4. The Period of Stagnation (1899-1925)

When we study the history of Zeme church, the period between 1899 to the years 1920s was a period of stagnation. P. T. Phillip also stated the church in this area did not enjoy a spectacular growth as in other parts of Nagaland.[115] This is chiefly because there was long silence with no establishment of new church for about 25 years. The Christians among these people were still less in number to have their own union. Efforts were being made by the native evangelists of the Angamis and the local Christians to evangelise this area. Angamis have been evangelising and by 1913 they sent a full time evangelist to work among this people. Yet, there was no furtherance of Christianity as there was neither a record of new convert nor the establishment of the new church other than these two churches of

113 *Benreu Baptist Church Diamond,* 15. *Cf.* Pame, *History of Zeliangrong Baptist Church in Nagaland,* 51.

114 Pame, *History of Zeliangrong Baptist Church in Nagaland,* 52

115 Phillip, *The Growth of Baptist Church in Nagaland,* 124.

Benreu in 1897 and Mpung in 1907. So the Zeme church remained under the Kohima Mission Field until 1926.[116]

3. Growth and the Formation of the Church

3.1. Union of Zeliang-Kuki Association, ZKA (1926-1953)

Although, the response by the Zeme to the Gospel was very poor with no record of any new church until 1925, many people from more villages embraced Christianity through the effort of native evangelists. This resulted to the establishment of the third church at Tening village lately in 1926. Soon few more Kuki churches were also found in the Zeliangrong area.[117] This then, paved a right way for the people to combine and work together since there were less Christians from both the tribes to stand on their own. Thus, two distinct tribes, the Zeliang and the Kuki Christians formed a joint association called Zelaing-Kuki Association (ZKA) in 1926 under the Kohima Mission Field.[118] In the same year 1926, shortly after the combine formation of association they separated from Kohima Field. It was rightly said that the Zeliang and the Kuki Christians of Nagaland had illustrated the spirit of ecumenism[119] and symbolized the type of church union although they represented different tribes and speak different languages, they joined together to foster each other so that the association could function with more members.

3.2. The New Period of Church Growth

Since the formation of the joint association with the Kukis, the growth of the churches was in balanced progress. Yet, on the other hand, there were also some factors operating in the Zeliangrong area

116 Downs, *The Mighty Works of God,* 124. *Cf.* Singson, "Kuki Baptist Association, (KBA)," in *From Darkness to Light,* edited by Alongla P. Aier (Kohima: NBCC, 1997), 74.

117 E. Zeliang, *Charismatic Movements,* 40.

118 Suitei, "Zeme Baptist Church Council, 90. *Cf. Zeliangrong Baptist Association Nagaland,* 8.

119 Haisuitei, "A Historical Study of Christianity and Heraka (*Kampai*) Cult among Zeliangrong People in Nagaland" (BD Thesis, United Theological College, 1989). 27.

that opposed Christianity with the influenced of Heraka Movement, adamant towards the new sentiments of faith. Alongside with, the Kuki Christians also faced persecution and were ill treated by the non-Christians.[120] Despite the problems which added to the slow growth, evangelists like Keneise and Ngulpu began to work as the first full time workers under the supervision of the Angami evangelists from Kohima Field through ZKA.[121] As the number of Christians increased, churches were slowly planted in other villages like Peren, Tening, Ntu, Tesen, Poilwa, etc.[122] The Zeliang is one of the biggest in Kohima district in terms of population, but had fewer Christians. The work is somewhat gradual and conversions are not many but once added to the church, they are found to be firm and earnest in their witnessing.

It is to be recorded that there were only eight churches in 1939 when Keneise was ordained by J. E. Tanquist as the first ordained minister among the Zeliang.[123] The early field workers like Keneise, Nheubuing, Turi, Ngulpu, Sojang, Wisung were working as representatives of the combined association to Kohima. Slowly as the number of Christians increased, a new mission school was established at Tesangki in Tesen, which was opened in 1944 through the initiation of evangelist Turi. This school run and functioned under the recognition of Government until the Kuki and Zeliang separated to form their own association.[124] In 1951, H. K. Lungalang was appointed as the first Field Director of the ZKA and during that time the record holds that there were only 14 churches of the Zeliang out of the 33 churches of the combined ZKA.[125] It was in

---

120 Downs, *The Mighty Works of God,* 124. *Cf.* Phillip, *The Growth of Baptist Church in Nagaland,* 117.

121 Pame, *History of Zeliangrong Baptist Church in Nagaland*, 62.

122 Name of the first converts are Kaithiu and Tashibe of Tening Village in 1926, Etingcung of Peren Village in 1927, Dizin of Tesen Village in 1928, Hugambo, Adiubo and Namkianglungbo of Ntu Village in 1928. From 1940-1950, Puiting and Isineung of Mhai, Hengalakpe of Ngwalwa, and others became Christian. *Cf. Benreu Baptist Church Centenary,* 52.

123 *Benreu Baptist Church Centenary*, 52-53.

124 Pame, *History of Zeliangrong Baptist Church in Nagaland*, 62.

125 E. Zeliang, *Charismatic Movements,* 41.

1953, that the Zeliang and the Kuki held their last annual session at Tesen Namci and parted to form their respective associations.[126] The Zeliang and the Kuki continued their combined association for almost three decades till 1953 and separated with good will for the simple reason of linguistic inconveniences.

3.3. Zeliang Baptist Association, ZBA (1953-1966)

Despite the predicament over the languages and cultures which cause many hindrances in collaborating missions between the Zeliang and Kuki, they had their combined Association for 28 years. Eventually in 1953, the Kuki felt the need of having their own association. It became imperative as they wanted to have their own literature after being conscious of the differences in culture and language. At the same time it also made them realised with understanding to divide and manage their own churches. Accordingly, the Zeliang also began to form their own association under the name Zeliang Baptist Association (ZBA), inclusive of both Zeme and Liangmai with H. K. Lungalang as the Field Director and Keneise and Turi as field evangelists. But the area is still laid for the proclamation of the gospel as many people were still non-Christians in many villages. After its separation from the Kuki, the first ZBA annual session was held at Ntu village in January, 8th-10th, 1954 with the addition of the new churches in the area.[127] Subsequently, in 1954 the association was recognised and affiliated to Nagaland Baptist Church Council[128] and her mission centre was momentarily established at Ndunglwa village. The nomenclature, Zeliang Baptist Association continued until 1966 before the insertion of Rongmais with their migration to Peren district.

---

126 *Tesen Baptist Nkwa Golden Jubilee Souvenir, 1928-1978* (Tesen: TBNGJ Committee, 1978), 3. *Cf.* Singson, "Kuki Baptist Association," 117.

127 Interview with Iriezeu Putlang, Ex-pastor, New Tesen Baptist Church, 12 October 2016.

128 *Zeliangrong Baptist Association Nagaland,* 8-11. *Cf.* Phuveyi Dozo, *The Growth of Baptist Churches in Chakhesang Naga Tribe (India)* (Kohima: Nagaland Missionary Movement, 1978), 102.

3.4. Establishment of Mission Centre

The Zeliang Christians after its separation from Kuki, felt the need of having their own mission centre primarily with an aim of doing mission through self-governing and self-supporting. So, there was a search of land suitable for the people in regard to surroundings, water, location and other concerns for its mission activities. Formerly, Peren was opted to be the centre of mission but location could not be procured due to disagreed consentient of the owner. So, for the convenience of the people in general, it was agreed that any place for mission centre should be 10 miles distance from Peren town. Likewise, a place was search near Jalukie town but because of the water problem, again it was shifted to Mbaulwa range and that too was failed as it was little far from Peren town. Finally, Ndunglwa was chosen to be the mission centre when the villagers willingly donated a tract of land to establish a mission centre.[129]

So, in 1954 the mission centre was first established at Ndunglwa with a pitiable condition of the building constructed with thatch as the office and quarters. By the end of 1955, there were only 21 churches with 637 baptised Christian. Few travelling pastors were seen who travelled from one village to another in order to help the churches in their work and worship.[130] Yet, the association was more dependent on the mission and accordingly, with the financial support from the Council of Baptist Churches in Assam and Manipur (CBCAM), a dispensary, a mission school and some translation of Gospel began. H. K. Lungalang continued to serve as the first full time Field Director and Keneise, Turi, Nheubuing were the full time evangelists of the association during that time.[131]

After much preparation with the infrastructures for further development, the problem arose because of the political issues during

129 Elungkiebe Zeliang, "Rev. Heizieding Kediteiheing Lungalang Teilung Ha, Personal Interview with Rev. H. K. Lungalang at his Residence at Ngwalwa village on 28 June, 1996," letter to the author, 15 November 2016.

130 Phillip, *The Growth of Baptist Church in Nagaland,* 125.

131 Suitei, "Zeme Baptist Church Council," 90-91. *Cf.* Pame, *History of Zeliangrong Baptist Church in Nagaland,* 64-65.

1954-56 between the insurgence group of Nagas and the Indian army. This problem was also coupled with travel inconveniences at Ndunglwa. So, after much negotiation it became necessary to shift the mission centre from Ndunglwa to the present location at Peren in 1958 as it finds more secure for the church and the people.[132]

4. Period of Significant Growth (1960-1982)

There was a growing period in the churches with remarkable changes during the period between 1960s to early 1970s. The main feature of this period was the wave of revival and literature. There was a wave of revival from 1976 that brought drastic changes in the life of the churches and as a consequence of the revival more evangelists were employed to propagate its home mission. Evangelists and church workers became more engaged in preaching and church planting and the Christian percentage rose from 60% to 90% during this period. Youth and Women departments were soon created in 1970 and various developmental works were established with the growth of the churches as its leadership.[133] Literature work has increased and the translation and printing of the Gospel, some booklets and tracts were made possible and translation of the entire New Testament also began which was released in 1982. Three schools were established within this period at Peren Town, Jalukie Town and Tening. Many non believers were converted and baptised. The report of H. K. Lungalang substantiated the there was significant growth during these period.

> 1965 is a year for us. For the last six or seven years the religious fanaticism under Rani Gaidinliu is troubling us. They eat, drink and dance and ... are opposed to Christianity, creating many troubles for our churches. But slowly and steadily we are increasing. During the year many were baptised of whom the majority were from the non-Christian background.[134]

---

132 Suitei, "Zeme Baptist Church Council," 90-91.

133 Suitei, "Zeme Baptist Church Council," 91.

134 H. K. Lungalang, "Zeliang Association," in *CBCNEI Sixteenth Annual Session, January 5-9* (Dimapur, Nagaland: n.p. 1966), 74.

The record holds that in 1966 the church membership grew up to 1100.[135] The report of 1968 also showed that the evangelists were accelerated and very active visiting the non-Christians with the Gospel of Jesus Christ, which as a result 98 new baptisms were made mostly from the non-Christians background.[136] With the growth of the churches and the villages in the Zeliangrong areas in 1960s, once again the Zeliang Baptist Association was changed to Zeliangrong Baptist Association (ZBA) in 1967 with a view to embrace more Christians with the migration of Rongmeis in Peren District.[137] During the years between the late 1970s to early 1980s, the church experienced a significant growth of proportion which brought changes in the nature and ministry of the church. By 1978 the members had increased to 5901 with 55 churches and in 1979 the ZBA could hold silver jubilee at Mission Centre, Peren Town, celebrating 25 years after its separation from the Zeliang-Kuki Association. Consequently in 1982 the ZBA churches had increased to 60 with as much as 15,000 Christians[138] with five ordained ministers.[139]

5. Dissemination of the Associations

The present nomenclature of the association that is, Zeme Baptist Church Council (ZBCC) had passed through different stages of growth and reduction. There were confusion and hurdles that ushered in, which led to the division of the associations among the Zeliangrongs as they emerged out from the ZBCC to form new association due to several inconveniences. The Zeliangrong Baptist Church was fragmented into three sub-associations mainly because of the dialectical divergence, where the congregation was

---

135 Phillip, *The Growth of Baptist Church in Nagaland,* 125.

136 H. K. Lungalang, "Zeliangrong Baptist Christian Association Report 1967," in *CBCNEI Eighteenth Annual Session, January 3-7* (Nishangram, Assam: n.p. 1968), 82.

137 Suitei, "Zeme Baptist Church Council," 90-91.

138 E. Zeliang, *Charismatic Movements,* 44.

139 The five ordained ministers are Rev. Keneise (1939), Rev. H. K. Lungalang (1955), Rev. Turi (1960), Rev. Hazieding (1973) and Rev. Lungzie (1982). *Benreu Baptist Church Centenary,* 46-51.

comprised of the three communities: the Zeme, the Liangmai and the Rongmai. The Liangmais in 1984, the southern Zeme in 1986, and the Rongmeis in 1988 separated and formed their respective associations. Eventually, the northern Zemes changed the name to Zeme Baptist Church Council which stands till today.[140] This division is mainly because of the inconveniences with regard to literature, communication and inconveniences in the administration of the church. However, there is oneness of the church in its ecumenical sense despite the division of the associations. Thereafter, begins the new story of Zeme Baptist Church Council with the separation of the Kuki Christians, the southern Zeme, Liangmai, Rongmai groups as discussed above from the combined association. Presently, the ZBCC has 67 churches with more than seventeen thousand baptised members and as much as sixteen thousand associate members with Izieteilung Terieng as the Executive Secretary.[141]

Conclusion

The Zeme people had in past, traditionally being different from their present life of what can be called after the coming of Christianity. The year 1897 was a landmark for the Zeme people primarily in the belief system after the conversion of Heizieluing, as it created a new history with the contact of new religion which had transformed the whole set up of the society and people. Educated from Kohima Mission School and became the first evangelist until his death. The coming of Christianity had affected the socio-economic, religious and cultural life of the people which continued to advance through the activities of missionaries and evangelists. The people were converted through simple preaching, singing, prayer and healing. It is also to be noted that the early Zeme converts were from the Kohima Field and nurtured by the native evangelists during the first stage of the Christianity. The newly converts were not properly accentuated to strong faith to maintain the standard of the Christian life from the beginning due to lack of trained leaders which probably is the reason

140 E. Zeliang, *Charismatic Movements,* 44.

141 Interview with Izieteilung Terieng, Executive Secretary, ZBCC Peren, 20 February 2017.

for slow growth of the churches then. On the other hand, the growth and the integrity of the church also had a measurable diminution with the coming out of different associations because of the linguistic and literature differences. Nevertheless, the traditional life of the people experienced a transformed society through the efforts of the indigenous leaders of the early converts. One can consider from darkness to light as the right description for the transition of the Zeme Nagas from their traditional belief system to the gospel of light.

3

Life Sketch of the Four Evangelists
A Biographical Study

Introduction

During the early period, it was a common feature of Christianity for converting and preaching, and evangelism has been constant through the efforts of the local evangelists. The story of the churches among the Zeme people began with the works of the dynamic local evangelists who gave and rendered their lives for the cause of their people by giving their utmost attention to evangelism. These dedicated pioneers faithfully took a firm stand to where they were called by the Lord and have proven by their works through whom, today the churches have the joy of bearing much fruits. Howard Houston who physically visited the area of this people remarked that people living in the shadow of mountains with few Christians and small churches was not easy. It stated that;

> It is difficult to be a Christian. It was our prayer that the villagers near the mountains might be won for the Lord

> Jesus Christ. That Prayer has been answered. Today the light of Christ shines around the mountain.[142]

It was in fact, inclusively through the conversions of the early Christians who have extensively worked in ground-breaking the Gospel during the initial period. This chapter will exclusively deal on the life and background of the four local evangelists among the many other genuine pioneers who have significantly contributed to the spread of the gospel among the people. They are namely- Rev. Keneise Meru, one of the early converts and the first ordained minister under ZBCC, Rev. H. K. Lungalang who worked extensively as the first Field Director of the association, Rev. Hazieding Hairangbuing, one of the first Field Evangelists of the Association and Evan. Wisungbo Nrak, an evangelist and a chief church planter who extensively engaged in pioneering the gospel and played a significant role towards the formation of Liangmai Baptist Association (LBA) in Nagaland.

1. Keneise Meru (1903-1962)

1.1. Early Life and Education

Keneise Meru was born into a family of the first convert among the Zeme. He was born on 15th December 1903 at Benreu village under Peren District, Nagaland. He was the grandson of Sozhumo, the founding father of Benreu village. His parent names were Heizieluing and Ndilule Meru. His father, Heizieluing was the first convert who established the first church among the Zeliangs and the first evangelist among the Kacha Naga (Zeme) people in Nagaland. Keneise was the third and the youngest son in the family. He appears not very tall with curvy legs, bald headed with curly hairs. He was brought up initially from Benreu village. He lost his father when he was only 15 years and was studying in Kohima.[143]

---

142 Houston, *Nagaland Adventure*, 1.

143 Interview with Rev. Kulungsing Meru, son of Rev. Keneise Meru, Ngwalwa village, 20 October 2016. *Cf.* S. Changsang, comp., *A Brief Life History of Naga Leaders in the 20th Century* (Kohima: The Directorate of Information and Public Relations, n.d.), 24.

Keneise did his education from Kohima Mission School and while he was studying in class VI, he quitted his education because of the disturbances of the World War-I and the epidemic that broke out during 1918.[144] Strangely, when the epidemic broke out, his father Heizieluing and his eldest brother Gwizao died in the same year in 1918, while his father was serving as pastor in village and his brother as headmaster at Impur Mission School (1915-1918). This compelled Keneise to return to his village from Kohima where he was studying leaving his educational career incomplete. His eldest brother Gwizao was also the first educated in the village who was considered to be brave and capable leader proved evidently from the many feats he accomplished during his student days at Shillong. Tragically, he died at Impur while his father died at village. Keneise, after returning home from Kohima, he got married in 1920 and was employed into a government service by the British Regime in Health Services as Vaccinator. But as it was God's will he responded to God's call and quitted his government job in 1926 and started working actively under the Kohima Field as evangelist.[145]

Like his eldest brother Gwizao, who was reported to be the translator of the hymnals,[146] Keneise was also a man who gave much hope to his people in serving and contributing with gifts in translating songs and Bible. It is also reportedly said that he was a good interpreter who could excellently interpret the evangelists' messages in the village, occasionally during his younger age which perhaps stimulated him to become evangelist.[147]

---

144 Interview with Rev. Kulungsing Meru, 20 October 2016.

145 Narola Rivenburg, ed., *The Star of the Naga Hills* (Chicago: Judson Press, 1941), 31. Interview with Rev. Kulungsing Meru, 20 October 2016.

146 His brother Gwizao was a pioneer in education and served as Headmaster at Impur Misssion School during 1915-1918. It is said that Gwizao had translated 12 songs of "Hymns in Kacha Naga," edited by J. E. Tanquist and published by American Foreign Mission Society at Kohima in 1918. *Benreu Baptist Church Diamond*, 14. *Cf.* Suitei Ndang, comp., *Zeme Baptist Church Council (N): Pe Rehah, Petah nah Pemacet-Mariem, 1910-2000* (Peren: Published by Compiler, 2002), 86. *Cf.* Changsang, *A Brief Life History of Naga Leaders in the 20th Century*, 24.

147 Rev. Kulungsing told that his father Rev. Keneise was a good interpreter during his time, who can read not only English Bible but also Akomia Bible

1.2. Marriage and Family Life

Keneise got married with Paurangyile in the year 1920. Significantly, their marriage program was held together along with three other couples on the same day at Benreu village. This marriage ceremony was solemnised by Heireilung, the second pastor of the first church among the Zeme area. God blessed Keneise and wife Paurangyile with seven children-three females and four males.[148]

Keneise was a man who sacrificed his life with exertion in evangelism for the Lord. He lived for 59 years and during his prime time of serving the Lord he was called for his eternal home. He passed away on 13th May 1962 not long after attending the Association Conference that was held on 5th - 7th January at Hainakui village in 1962.[149] His wife Paurangyile lived as a widow for about 30 years and died on one of the days of ZBCC council days on 31st January 1991. Keneise and wife Paurangyile were devoted God servants with much zeal to work for God. Keneise although his life was short, his ministry was full and fruitful leaving a great legacy to his people.

1.3. Work Prior to His Ordination

Prior to his ordination in 1939, Keneise and others from the association have been working actively as evangelists since 1926 under Kohima Field and they were paid by the Kohima Mission Field [150] Although he was not yet a licentiate minister to perform any Christian ordinances, he used to baptise and had his converts as he was commissioned to administer baptism and also solemnised holy marriages and funeral ceremonies. This commission was usually given because of the lack of native pastors or evangelists during those days. He was an evangelist working under Kohima Field and later when the Kohima Field Church Council was held in 1939 at Benreu, he was ordained by J. E. Tanquist and became the first ordained

---

(Assamese). Interview with Rev. Kulungsing Meru, 20 October 2016.

148 Interview with Rev. Kulungsing Meru, 20 October 2016.

149 *Zeliangrong Baptist Association Nagaland,* 14.

150 *Baptist Mission Church Kohima Centenary Souvenir-1885-1985* (Kohima: KMC, 1985), 1.

minister of the Zeme association.[151] He was ordained for full time gospel ministry and served as an evangelist for many years in the area until his death.

1.4. Keneise during the Zeliang-Kuki Association

Prior to 1926, there were only a handful of local leaders who worked actively as evangelists among the Zeliang people during the time when the Zeliang people were under the Kohima Field. However, due to the tireless efforts of the early Christians that by 1926 a new leader name Keneise was called by God to work and evangelise the people. It is believed to be accounted to Keneise when the report of J. E. Tanquist in 1927 says;

> Among the Zeme, where we have had worked for many years have employed no evangelists since the death of the faithful preacher several years ago. We now have a good high school trained young man, who while he is in government service is zealous for the evangelisation of his own people ... this should prove the greatest value for the evangelisation of the tribe.[152]

Keneise along with Turi were the lone evangelists from the Zeliang working along with the other evangelist like Ngulpu, during the ZKA.[153] Those days when there was a combined association with Kuki, they used to have communication problem as they speak different languages. However, he is said to have the gift of interpreting the messages as he toured around the area with other evangelists and interpreted the sermons of other evangelists. He travelled the whole area of both Zeliang and Kuki converting and baptising the new converts[154] and within few years of time many villages were reached with Christianity. There are also many instances where he called people with burden to work for God besides simply converting and baptising. He worked in several ministries such as

151 *Benreu Baptist Church Centenary*, 26.

152 *Zeliangrong Baptist Association Nagaland Silver*, 2.

153 Pame, *History of Zeliangrong Baptist Church in Nagaland*, 62.

154 Interview with Rev. Kulungsing Meru, 20 October 2016.

a pastor, evangelist, member of a board, treasurer, president, etc., during the combine association.[155]

Due to lack of record during the period 1926-1951, not much information were found about the work. However, after the separation with the Kukis, Keneise partnered with Turi as the main pillars initiated the evangelistic work visiting the villages along with their friends like Nheubuing Nsarangbe, Lungzie, Deuhing, Hazieding. They have toured every village with a burden to share the good news. Sometimes, they have to face severe persecution experiencing many difficulties when the villagers do not permit to enter their village. Instrumentally, he was an evangelist under Kohima Field and devoted his time as a missionary in nurturing the new converts and fellowshipping with the early Christians by visiting every Zeliang area.

1.5. His Wife Paurangyile (1900-1991)

Paurangyile, the wife of Keneise was a daughter of Diranglung. Her father was a village Gaun bura and served as one of the first deacons of the church.[156] Paurangyile, being the daughter of a deacon was a devoted, God fearing woman. In the midst of her many non Christian friend circles she remained faithful in her relationship with God. She was born in the year 1900 and was three years older to her husband. Although she could not get proper formal education, she could fluently read and speak Angami, which was the first introduced literature and common language. She could read and knew properly the Bible stories which helped her to teach Bible and missionaries stories to her children, showing perfect example of a good Christian woman and laid a strong foundation to her children's lives in spite of her limited educational knowledge.[157]

Those days Benreu, which is her native village was a strong *Renet* village (non-Christian) where every household had rice beer. To give up their ancient belief which was deeply rooted in their customs

155 *Zeliangrong Baptist Association Nagaland*, 12-19. *Cf.* Ndang, *Zeme Baptist Church Council*, 14.

156 *Benreu Baptist Church Centenary*, 28.

157 Interview with Rev. Kulungsing Meru, 20 October 2016.

and practices was looked upon with hostility. She therefore, prudent and ideal in nature prayed often for her children and advised them so that they are not influenced by the practices of those who follow traditional religion. Her husband, who was working as evangelist under the association was very busy and rarely stays at home because of his ministry in evangelizing the people. Even when he stayed at home, he was occupied in an isolated room in translating the Bible. Thus, she played her role as a good house-keeper and a teacher of her family as equal as that of her husband. She was a prayerful mother and most of the time her children will see her knees down and praying.[158] She lived as a widow for about 30 years after her husband left her in 1962. Even at her advancing age she continued to uphold the charge of Christian witness to others faithfully. She had been a blessing to the village as elderly woman until she passed away on 31st January 1991.[159]

2. Heizieding Kediteiheing Lungalang (1919-2010)

2.1. Early Life and Education

Heizieding Kediteiheing (Kevizelie) Lungalang, popularly known as H. K. Lungalang was the eldest son of Epetlung and Heirangswale Lungalang. His father Epetlung served as Dobashi in Kohima during 1918. Yet in the early part of 1919 he returned back to serve as a teacher at Benreu village which he continued till 1947. Later on, he rose to become the Bench Court Chairman of Zeliang-Kuki Tribal Council which was considered to be equivalent to the post of first class magistrate. Government servant by profession, yet he was part and parcel of the church and society. He also served as Sunday school superintendent for many years and was even appointed as Relief Treasurer of the Zeliangrong Association. He lived an exemplary life contributing and sacrificing for the church and society. As such the Church compound of Benreu Baptist Church which was donated

---

158 Kulungsing testified that her mother always prays before she does anything both outside and inside the house. Her prosperous children today are the part and parcel of her prayerful mother. Interview with Rev. Kulungsing Meru, 20 October 2016.

159 *Benreu Baptist Church Diamond,* 19.

by him still stands to testify his philanthropic work.[160] Further this legacy was brought forward to a greater height when his son Lungalang committed his life to serve the Lord.

Lungalang was born in October 1919 at Benreu village. He was the eldest child amongst the six children of his parents. Being the eldest, he was cognizant of his responsibility and hence was obedient to his parents.[161] He began his early education at Government Primary School Benreu and later he had the privileged of studying in different institutions unlike most of his peer groups. He studied at Mission Training School, Kohima (MTS) till class VI and was baptised in the year 1933 by Zapuzülie. During that time George William Supplee was the principal and Rezükhrie was the headmaster of the school.[162] He then shifted to Government High School, Shillong from 1937-1941 and studied till class X. Lungalang was an ambitious student who aspired to become a medical doctor so he joined the Cotton College, Guwahati in 1943 for Intermediate of Science Course (ISC/PU Science) with additional subject in biology. But unfortunately, in his 2nd year due to sudden outbreak of World War-II, all the examination papers were either burnt or damaged and the information was given that the re-examination would be scheduled for another time. However, due to poor communication in those days, he and his friends could not receive the information on time. It was unfortunate for some of his classmates and him as they were unable to obtain their result. Therefore, he had to discontinue his Intermediate of Science Course.[163] Despite the unfavourable and disagreeable events of fate he met, he remain undeterred, so he went

---

160 E. Zeliang, "Rev. Heizieding Kediteiheing Lungalang Teilung Ha," 15 November 2016.

161 H. K. Lungalang day of birth was not known because of the lack of record during those days but he was said to have born during the time of first harvesting ceremony in the village, probably in the early part of October. "Rev. H. K. Lungalang, Leaving Permanent Footprints," in *One New Humanity in Christ: Nagaland Baptist Church Council celebrates Platinum Jubilee 1937-2012* (Kohima: Documentation and Publication Committee, NBCC, 2012), 187.

162 E. Zeliang, "Rev. Heizieding Kediteiheing Lungalang Teilung Ha," 15 November 2016.

163 "Rev. H. K. Lungalang, Leaving Permanent Footprints," 187.

ahead to pursue Intermediate Science course in Mathematics from St. Anthony's College, Shillong where he passed out in 1945.[164] In 1953 he joined Jorhat Mission School to attend theological training for one year during an era when Duffy was the principal of the school. And it is very interesting to mention that, along with his basic theological training he was asked to be a tutor for class-10 students because of his efficiency in mathematics. He also had the privileged of attending the Ao Baptist Diamond Jubilee in 1953. Indeed because of this short course of theology that he undertook in 1953 at Jorhat Mission School, people regarded him as a theologically trained person.[165]

2.2. Institutional Involvement

Lungalang after his education from Shillong in 1945, was appointed as the headmaster/teacher of John Institute during its inception, (then a middle school) during 1945-1946 in Viswema village. It is now upgraded to John Government Higher Secondary School. In 1947, he joined government service as the headmaster of Government Middle School in Phek, appointed by the Government of Assam.[166] In 1948, he was transferred to Kohima Government High School as assistant teacher and in the later part of the same year, he went to undergo Basic Education Training (BET) at Servagram, Uttar Pradesh as trainee for 9 months and completed in 1949. After completing the BET, he returned and joined the same school. However, he was again transferred to Tura by Kalita, the then headmaster, so he stayed in Tura from January to March 1951 and served until he resigned in May 1951 from the government service to serve the Zeliangrong Baptist Churches. By that time his salary has increased to Rs. 75 with allowance of Rs. 100.[167] Despite of the many privileges that he was enjoying being a government servant, he

---

164 E. Zeliang, "Rev. Heizieding Kediteiheing Lungalang Teilung Ha," 15 November 2016.

165 Interview with Rev. Kulungsing Meru, 20 October 2016.

166 Interview with Mteiziu Lungalang, son of Rev. H. K. Lungalang, Ngwalwa village, 27 October 2016.

167 "Rev. H. K. Lungalang, Leaving Permanent Footprints," 187.

did not give a second thought to response to the call that came like a 'Macedonian Call.'[168] Hence, after a brief stint of his involvement in schools and government service, sensing the need of an educated people to lead the Zeliangrong churches in general and Zeme churches in particular, he left his comfort Zone.

2.3. Marriage and Ordination

Lungalang married Rangmeuheile, on 28th March 1952, solemnized by Keneise and coincidently Kulungsing son of Keneise blessed their 50th year of marriage ceremony in 2002. They were blessed with four children-three daughters and one son, though one daughter predeceased them.[169] He was ordained by R. F. Delano, the last American Missionary in the presence of Keneise Meru and N. Savino on Sunday, 16th January 1955 during the ZBA conference at Peren Town.[170]

Prior to his ordination, beginning from 1951, he was already appointed as the field Director of ZKA and during such time a transition was taking place in the mission field, because an order was passed by the government that a missionary by the name Houston should leave Nagaland. In such a scenario, Anderson was recalled back from Sumi area to come over to Kohima Field. Then, Kohima Field being the caretaker of the ZKA, Lungalang seized this opportunity to associate himself with Anderson and it is said that Anderson and his wife attended the ZKA in January 1952 at Heningkunglwa.[171] The Lord blessed and used his faithful servant in the Zeme churches who profoundly contributed to his people leaving a great legacy until he left to be with the Lord on 31th January 2010.

---

168 H. K. Lungalang, "Zeliang-Kuki Association-Naga Hills," in *Council of Baptist_Churches in Assam, Second Session, December 29 1951-January 5 1952* (Nowgong, Assam: n.p. 1952), 46.

169 Interview with Mteiziu Lungalang, 27 October 2016.

170 Lungalang, "Apau Dade Raukelu Document," 28 October 2016.

171 E. Zeliang, "Rev. Heizieding Kediteiheing Lungalang Teilung Ha," 15 November 2016.

2.4. Ministerial Experiences

Lungalang also served the Nagaland Baptist Church Council (NBCC) as President from 1961 to 1963.[172] He was also part of the NBCC Peace Committee alongside Longri Ao, Kenneth Kerhuo and others, which was set up in 1964 to broker peace between Federal Government of Nagaland (FGN) and Government of India (GOI). In this journey of seeking peace for the Nagas, he was also closely associated with B. P. Chaliha, the then Chief Minister of Assam, Jayaprakash Narayan, a veteran freedom fighter and Michael Scott, a popular missionary from England.[173]

He also served as the Administrator of Christian Higher Secondary School, Dimapur from 1976 to 1981. He served as the pastor of Ngwalwa Baptist Church from 1982 to 1984. After which due to the absence a potential candidate to lead the Association, he was re-appointed as Executive Secretary of ZBCC for a period of two years 1987-1988.[174] He has contributed all his abled days striving forth for Christ not escaping the call of God.

2.5. Brief Profile of Mrs. Rangmeuheile Lungalang

Rangmeuheile Lungalang was born in and around 1930's at Benreu village. She was the second daughter and third child of Lungleudaule and Rangchauheing Thou. She did her basic education and spent her childhood at Benreu village. She got married to Lungalang on 28th march 1952. After her marriage, she accompanied her husband and settled in different places taking care of their children and helping her husband in his ministry.[175] Even though it was not so convenient for a family to move to different places, she managed to cope up with the demand of her husband's ministry. At times, she also had to shoulder the responsibilities of her home alone when her husband had to go for long tour visiting different places for his ministry. Despite all

---

172 "Rev. H. K. Lungalang, Leaving Permanent Footprints," 187.

173 V. K. Nuh, *50 Years of Peace Work by Nagaland Churches and Naga Civil Societies* (Dimapur: FNBA, 2014), 35-37.

174 E. Zeliang, "Rev. Heizieding Kediteiheing Lungalang Teilung Ha," 15 November 2016.

175 Interview with Mteiziu Lungalang, 27 October 2016.

these, she never failed to impute the word of God to her children and brought them up with proper education to live a dignified life. She was indeed the driving force that helped her husband to strive forth working for the Lord. Though she did not have much education as usual to many women then, she could read the vernacular Bible which enabled her to help her husband in his ministry. Generous by nature, she never failed to feed a hungry soul and share her blessings and humble resources with people around her. She was a woman who loved to share the gospel and her experiences of working with the Lord. As often as she could, she would encourage the church workers who came to her through her experiences of how the Lord has blessed her even in the midst of disappointments, encountering helpless situations, quoting the biblical text, "the Lord will take care of those He has called and will never let them grow hungry." Beside these, she would spend her time praying and reading the Bible together with her husband. A strict guardian of culture and tradition, she would always insist that her children and grandchildren uphold traditional values passed down through generation. She spent all her life working for the Lord alongside her husband until death separated them. Even after the death of her husband she took every possible opportunity to serve the Lord in a humble way to carry forward the legacy left behind by her husband. She served in the church in different capacities and associated with it until she breathe her last on 8th August 2012, three years after the death of her husband. She exhibited a caring and loving life which was worth emulating. She longed and advocated for a loving relationship amongst her family and she stood for humanitarian work.[176]

3. Hazieding Hairangbuing (1922-1997)

3.1. Early Life

Hazieding was born into a non-Christian family of Heidwalung and Lungtaheile Hairangbuing. He was born in the year 1922 at Benreu village and had four brothers and one sister. Then, his father was a

176 Interview with Epetlung Lungalang, D. Th. student, UTC Bangalore, 20 November 2016.

believer of Rani Gaidinliu.[177] He did his early schooling from his village under Epetlung Lungalang during 1932-1936 and studied up to class IV. However, due to the absence of educational institution in the area, he went to Kohima to continue with his studies and studied up to class V standard.[178] Although, he was not highly educated, he was an active, strong and a typical youth with great ambitions to be successful in the line of the work of his choice. He spent his youth limited much within the village serving and working as a village secretary. The reason he could not get proper education could be because he was born into a non-Christian family whose customs and belief are ingrained so much to their traditional life and had ignored the education. Despite his low class he could fluently read and write for preaching and teaching the Bible stories to the people.[179]

3.2. Marriage and Conversion

Leisiuzeule, the fourth daughter of Deusamheing was the wife of Hazieding. They got married in the month of February 1944, before his conversion. After his marriage he involved in Naga National Council (NNC) Youth among the Zeliangrong region during 1946-1949 as the Treasurer.[180] As responsible parents, he and his wife were challenged and discouraged many times with deep experiences of losing their children, of which only three are alive today.[181] He spent his life without knowing Christ for around 30 years in the environment of Christian influence until he accepted Christ as his personal Saviour. He lived a life of his choice but God had different plan for him. One day he felt the call upon him by God and was

177 Interview with Rev. Deuhing Nsa, Former Evangelist, Peren Town, 25 October 2016. He is 97 years old and one of the earliest evangelists in the Zeme area.

178 Elungkiebe Zeliang, "Rev. Hazieding Teilung Ha, Personal Interview with Rev. Hazieding at his House at Heningkunglwa on 30 June, 1996," letter to the author, 15 November 2016.

179 Interview with Kedileuheing, son of Rev. Hazieding, Ngwalwa village, 2 November 2016.

180 E. Zeliang, "Rev. Hazieding Teilung Ha," 15 November 2016.

181 They had eleven children with four sons and eight daughters however eight of their children died and they have three children alive by name of Itingumle, Khriengusano and Kedileuhing.

made realised to know the worth of soul and the eternal dividends to inherit if he give his life whole heartedly to the Lord and work for his kingdom. Accordingly, not long after his marriage he accepted Christ as his personal Saviour in the month of February 1952 and in the following year he received water baptism through Keneise on 1st June 1953. Following him, his wife also got baptised on 1st June 1954.[182]

Prior to his conversion, he was often seen at the porch of his house with his rice beer cup but later on he was often seen travelling from village to village preaching the love of God.[183] His wife Leisiuzeule was also a devoted woman of faith and worked actively in the church as deaconess for many years and died on 16th May 1987 at Heningkunglwa. After his wife left him for her heavenly abode, he continued serving the Lord and lived for 76 years until his last breath on 7th July 1997 while he was on his evangelical ministry in Jalukie-B at Deukoram and buried at Ngwalwa.[184] Hazieding, though was a recent convert, developed a firm faith and grew enthusiastic to work for God among his people. As young as his faith was, in no time after his conversion from February 1952 he travelled around from place to place in the Zeliangrong area in the business of the Lord doing evangelistic work.

3.3. Evangelistic Ministry

Hazieding began his ministry by working in the Kohima Field as the Church Council Member through the Kacha Naga Association (this refer to the Association of Zeliang) during 1953-1954 along with pastor Wisungbo of Tening Baptist Church. After a service of two years in Kohima Field he returned to his village and served there as deacon for a year. Hazieding was a man who earnestly walked and worked for God travelling from one place to another along with

182 This record is written on a memorial stone by his son Kedileuhing at Ngwalwa village. Information is also found that he was the first Christian among the Rau khel from Benreu village. Personally, researcher visited the place on 22 October 2016.

183 Interview with Rev. Kulungsing Meru, 20 October 2016.

184 Interview with Leusi Meyase, Pastor, Ngwalwa Baptist Church, 20 October 2016.

other evangelists. Even before he was called by the association, he along with Keneise have preached to several villages including the neighbouring villages like Maova, Socunoma, Mulbung, Hepunglwa (now called Punglwa village), Gaili, Ngwalwa and others.[185]

While he was serving in his village he was called by the ZBA on 4th April 1956 to Poilwa village to be a mission pundit for one year. So, he served at Poilwa as mission teacher with a responsibility of looking after the church that had only two Christian households and a widow with a payment of Rs. 15 through the sponsorship of ZBA and Mr. Kedileung pay for him Rs. 5, so he received Rs. 20 monthly. During this time, Mr. Diteung was serving as pastor at Poilwa Baptist Church. After one year ministry at Poilwa he returned to his villages to give his service to his own villagers 1957. However, God wanted to use him in a broader ministry and accordingly he was sent to Punglwa village as mission pundit by the Council of ZBA on 4th March 1958. By this time his salary was increased to Rs. 30 per-month for the pundit work and in 1959 Mr. Heileuding, father of Lamswa was installed as Pastor in Punglwa.[186] While serving in Punglwa, one day they were on the way to Ghaspani to buy a buffalo for the festival that was going to be held at Benreu. Unfortunately, he and Heiriakieng were wrongly accused by the Maova (Kuki) village guards suspecting them as spies with a false report that they were working for NNC and on their journey to buy things for them. There they were beaten severely and jailed them for one month at Kohima Central Jail in May 1959. After he was released from the fateful incident he was employed as peon (1059-1961, two years) under Dopenga during the time when Mrs. Khrunuo was the ADC in Kohima. So, Hazieding along with his whole family shifted to Kohima. However, needing his service after the death of Mr. Heileuding who served as pastor at Punglwa, request came again for his service in the area since there was less evangelists. So Mr. Nsimlakpe and Mr. Pauheidiakpe were sent to Kohima to call him back. Leaving some of his properties to Dopenga, he returned

185 Kedileuheing, "Rev. Hazieding Bata Ha Rau Mdui Kegai," letter to the author, 4 November 2016.

186 Kedileuheing, "Rev. Hazieding Bata Ha," 4 November 2016.

and served as pastor at Punglwa in 1962. While he was serving as pastor, Angami Women Department through ZBA sponsored him with monthly payment of Rs. 100 to work as pastor and evangelist in Zeliang area. So he served as pastor and evangelist for five years during 1962-1967 in the area nurturing the Christians and tending the new flocks. In 1967 when Mr. Hiacau was appointed as new pastor at Punglwa, he continued as evangelist in the area and this time he was sponsored by Mr. Mhalie, the then Field Director of Angami Association for one year in 1968.[187] According to his personal record, he had an unrest evangelistic ministry in the whole Zeliang area stationed in different villages until 1971. From 1969-1970 he was sponsored by Mr. Epetlung Lungalang with monthly salary of Rs. 250 for evangelism. Progressive and productive in his ministry, from 1971 till December 1986 he was once again appointed as Field Evangelist by the ZBCC. After working for many years as evangelist he was ordained at Gaili during the Association Conference on 4th February 1973.[188]

Hazieding seized all the opportunity to evangelise his people until he himself considered to retire as he grew advanced in age. So, in 1983, Turi and he appealed the ZBCC during the Annual Council at Kezanglwa to release them since they crossed 60 years but their request was refused. Again in 1985 at Nzauna on Annual Council day he made a same request to release from the field evangelistic work but he was requested to extent his ministry until December 1986 from the Association.[189]

3.4. His Record of Baptism and Marriage Ceremony

Year	No. of Persons he Baptised	No. of Marriages
1973	96	4
1974	87	4
1975	113	3
1976	264	11

187 E. Zeliang, "Rev. Hazieding Teilung Ha," 15 November 2016.

188 Kedileuheing, "Rev. Hazieding Bata Ha," 4 November 2016.

189 E. Zeliang, "Rev. Hazieding Teilung Ha," 15 November 2016.

1977	971	13
1978	398	8
1979	96	7
1980	97	5
1981	57	7
1982	76	8
1983	29	3
1984	86	3
1985	105	4
1986	117	2
1987	15	1
1988	10	1
1989	21	2
1990	36	2
1991	84	7
1992	82	3
1993	105	1
1994	115	2
1995	50	2
1996		3
TOTAL	**3110 Members**	**106** (93 Holy Marriage, 13 Home Marriage)

3.5. His Highest Record of Baptism

Village	Date	No. of Baptism
1. Peren Town Crusade	21st Oct. 1977	113
2. Jalukie Town Crusade	11th Dec. 1977	126+9[190]=135
3. New Jalukie, ZBCC Association	29th Jan. 1978	116

According to his personal record, Hazieding, thereafter his ordination he solemnised the first Holy Marriage ceremony to Mr. Achigwangmang, son of Kairisiyang of New Jalukie and Miss Guiningliu on 14th March 1973. He had worked for 3812 days during his evangelical years under ZBCC since his ordination. He had ministered the Lord Supper 991 times, dedicated 22 churches and 31 pastors besides home dedication, memorial stone and deacon dedication.[190]

Hazieding after retiring as field evangelist for three years from the ZBCC, he again served as Project Evangelist of the association from 1991 to 1995. By this time he could experience the seed he had sowed to the churches few decades ago. The churches that he served fervently once were now sponsoring him. He was sponsored by Poilwa church in commemoration of their Golden Jubilee with a payment of 1100-1150 per month. In 1996, he also again served as home evangelist visiting homes and families in Heningkunglwa village at the request of the church to nurture and encourage the Christians for the celebration of Golden Jubilee. Even at his old age he zealously served the Lord visiting homes and evangelising the individuals and churches until his death in 1997.[191]

4. Wisungbo Nrak (1901-1977)

4.1. Early Life

Wisungbo was born into a poor non-Christian family at Tening village on 4th July 1901.[192] His father's name was of Chehotpuibo who resides in Tening Village. From his childhood he had hurdled so many problems and grew up under the care of his father after his mother died when he was a small boy. Since he was from a poor family, he often faced low regard on himself and had a sense of inferiority complex as he was neglected and looked down by the people. His own family problem with his poor health added with poor eyesight (partially blind) had a murky childhood. He was

190 Kedileuheing, "Rev. Hazieding Bata Ha," 4 November 2016.

191 Kedileuheing, "Rev. Hazieding Bata Ha," 4 November 2016.

192 Interview with Maithongphung Newmai, grandson of Wisungbo, Pastor, Zeliangrong Baptist Church, Chumukedima, 27 August 2020.

physically differently abled unlike his friends, who always had his walking stick to be an adjunct to wherever he goes. This blind feature made him look shabby and clumsy for which people mocked and made fun of him. Unlike any other children, he does not have any record of formal education as his family was very poor and his health was not as strong as other children who could easily go to school. Therefore, Wisungbo's childhood was with many struggles of tears and perspiration.[193]

4.2. Conversion and Baptism

Wisungbo was the first convert among the Tening Village (Henima) Baptist Church, converted probably during 1926. Before his conversion, Wisungbo was often confronted with depression and discouragement. He had many moments of being ignored and rejected by the people. Yet, though the world ignored him, God in his mercy and grace picked him up and chose him as His mighty instrument. He heard the message of Christ and the love of God through the evangelist Rev. Ngulpu and accepted Christ in 1926. After some time of his conversion, he accepted Jesus Christ as his personal Saviour and took an oath of baptism on 12th Dec. 1927.[194]

Wisungbo was one of the first converts among the Liangmais. He was the founder of Tening Baptist Church and became the first pastor. Later he played an important role in the formation of Liangmai Baptist Association (LBA) in Nagaland.[195] He was also one of the first evangelists among the Zeliang and Kuki during the combined association with the Kukis for his whole life time committing fifty years of his life in the service of the Lord.[196]

---

193 *Tening Village Baptist Church Platinum Jubilee 1925-2000* (Tening: TVPJ Committee, 2000), 16; Pamei, *The Zeliangrong Nagas*, 57. *Cf.* Alice Chewang, "Historical Study on the Impact of Christianity upon the Role and Status of Liangmai Women from 1925 till the Present Time" (M.Th. Thesis, Eastern Theological College, 2013), 59.

194 *Tening Village Baptist Church Platinum Jubilee 1925-2000* (Tening: TVPJ Committee, 2000), 16; Pamei, *The Zeliangrong Nagas*, 57.

195 Ramriwang, "Liangmai Baptist Association (LBA)," in *From Darkness to Light,* edited by Alongla P. Aier (Kohima: NBCC, 1997), 75.

196 *Tening Village Baptist Church Platinum*, 15.

However insignificant he was in his education, his evangelism among the people during his life time was significant which resulted to a numerous growth of Christianity.

It is remarkable to mention that inspite of his physical disability as born being partially blind, he travelled extensively unlike others to gain ample knowledge of Bible so that he could share the word of God with his people in effect. He could neither read nor write but it is said that he had an extra-ordinary memory power. So he went up to Kohima to learn the Bible and songs (mostly Angami's dialect) which later enabled him to cite and quote many Bible verses and stories accurately while preaching the gospel.[197] Wisungbo was an effective servant of God who despite his illiteracy and poor health seized all the circumstances in the mission of God from his conversion till his death. He was coupled with an affectionate and gentle woman by name Leipuang, who always encouraged him whenever he came home sad and dejected.[198] They had no children of their own yet, God blessed them with tender hearts to care and love children besides their interests with the youth and women. He served as an evangelist and pastors his whole life making a record of 50 years and died on 21st July 1977 at Tening village.[199] Wisung although uneducated, was one of the most influential men among the Liangmai people in the early days of Christianity.

4.3. Evangelistic Ministry

After his baptism in 1927, he took up the challenge of sharing the gospel to his own people and in the neighbouring villages to whomever he could contact doing evangelism work. In 1933, Adinbou and his friends from Ntu village heard of his gospel message and became Christians.[200] As he gained his converts, he was hated by his relatives and they persecuted and despised him to stay outside

197 Interview with Iriezeu Putlang, Ex-pastor, New Tesen Baptist Church, 24 October 2016. *Cf.* Ramriwang, "Liangmai Baptist Association," 75.

198 Interview with K. Lailu Nrak, Pastor, Tening Village Baptist Church, 24 January 2017.

199 Chewang, "Historical Study on the Impact of Christianity," 60. *Cf. Liangmai Baptist Aruang Silver Jubilee Souvenir 2009* (LBASJ Committee, 2009), 53.

200 Pamei, *The Zeliangrong Nagas,* 57.

of the village. Since Wisungbo and few converts could not live in the village because of the opposition by the people, they made their dwelling in the outskirts of the village area and made a small hut and started their worship service. Fighting against all odds, he converted many souls travelling to different villages and gradually he established a church at Tening in 1927 which became the first church of the Liangmais in Nagaland.[201] As he continued to serve the Lord faithfully, he received a financial help of Rs. 5 from Miss Heipei of Tesen village and Ntu Baptist Church. While preaching in the nearby villages, he slept in granaries and in the jungle because he was not allowed to sleep in the village and refused to offer him food and water. However this did not discourage him rather he prayed for them and continued to evangelise them. Meanwhile, a good number of people accepted Christianity.[202] During the time when the Zeliang had combined association with the Kukis, Wisung worked as a field worker under the association in the Kohima Field as the Church Council Member through the association during 1953-1954 along with pastor Hazieding. Again from 1957 to 1959, he worked as mission pundit and evangelist in the Zeliang area.[203]

Conclusion

It is in fact true that in any particular context when the gospel was first presented, there used to be hostile attitude by the non-Christians towards their fellow friends and relatives who had embraced Christianity, especially in the context of the Nagas. It was difficult to leave one's own traditional belief system and follow new religion because they were persecuted and forsaken by their family and village. However, these committed servants of God remained true and firm in their faith. One can imagine how the Zeme churches have reach thus far through the lives of the pioneer evangelists in course of gospel promulgation.

---

201 "Wisung: A Pioneering Pastor," in *One New Humanity in Christ: Nagaland Baptist Church Council celebrates Platinum Jubilee 1937-2012* (Kohima: Documentation and Publication Committee, NBCC, 2012), 182.

202 *Liangmai Baptist Aruang Silver,* 20.

203 Kedileuheing, "Rev. Hazieding Bata Ha," 4 November 2016.

The evangelists have come a long way coupled with the help of their wives under recommendation who allow them to leave the comfort of their homes for the cause of their own people. It is apparent that their wives also shouldered equal responsibility along with their men despite socio-cultural attitude in the traditional family and society. Frequent itinerant evangelism of their husbands would leave them to kneel in prayers for their men at the same time take care of their family, children and other household chores. However limited it may be, it has been briefly highlighted from the above discussion and plainly present the life and background of these prominent servants of God. These people from their humble beginning as evangelists worked diligently with unflinching service for the sake of the gospel. They unwearyingly laboured with zealous hearts which is commendable. Their immense work of evangelistic efforts with strong determination resulted to transformation of the churches.

4

Works and Contributions of the Evangelists

Introduction

Having presented the Life Sketch and the background of the evangelists in the previous chapter, this chapter will present how their contributions have shaped the Zeme Churches in the growth and formation of the churches and brought significant impact in the society. Glancing through the biography of the pioneers who champion the cause of Christ in Zeliang area, it is obvious that the Zeliang pioneer evangelists encountered several hurdles. Yet they were not shaken neither were they discouraged by the hindrances and hardships. They were rather enthusiastic and triggered off exceedingly to share the Good News to their own people and even beyond their own tribe. Zealous and committed as the apostles in the early church history they endeavoured to spread the gospel to all the Zeme inhabited areas. Walking the extra miles with no formal theological training they could reach out and convinced their people to embrace Christ. It was indeed a herculean task to convince the people who were deeply rooted in their traditional beliefs.

In this ambitious mission of spreading the gospel, native evangelists from other tribes have also immensely contributed for the growth of Christian population. Nevertheless, major parts of entire Zeme area was evangelised with strong conviction by the early local converts and evangelists who remained firm to their new-found faith. Thus, this chapter is an attempt to bring out their contributions towards the society.

1. Concept of Pioneering Evangelism

To understand better the works and contributions of the Zeme local evangelists, it is imperative to analyse and understand the meaning and concept of pioneering evangelism. Thus, the writer proposes two phases of evangelistic perspective of the pioneers.

1.1. Pioneering Evangelism

Pioneering evangelism can be simply understood by comparing the life and ministry of Jesus who came to this earth. He came and proclaimed the good news of love, healed the sick and at the same time faced oppositions, persecutions and he was crucified. Yet, he fulfilled the purpose of God. It is a pioneering evangelism when the missionaries enters into any new unreached culture and starts evangelism, following the example of Jesus.[204] Similarly, the entering of the missionaries into the Naga Hills then, was in hostile condition and the peril of the life was eminent because they were being opposed by the animistic people who were also known as headhunters then. These missionaries started their pioneering role in a very insignificant manner with steady growth. It was a pioneering work followed by the evangelisation as a result by local converts. Thus, the legacy of pioneering work done by the missionaries was impacted to the early native converts for evangelisation to their own tribesmen.

---

204 Phuveyi Dozo, *Hill Tribes Now for Tribes in India: A Challenge for Evangelization* (Calcutta: NMM: Nagaland Baptist Church Council, n.d.), 21.

1.2. Local Evangelism

Local evangelism is evangelisation by the local converts who continue the process of witnessing for Christ after their conversion like the Samaritan woman telling of Christ after she met Christ.[205] The early Zeliang evangelists after their conversion through the missionaries continued the same process of evangelising the people. Being consumed by their great concern for the conversion and calling people to Christ, they had actively involved in evangelistic task that without any official missionary assistance, they could transform the lives of the people towards Christ. This should get high priority in the life, plan and program of the individuals and its churches. Pettigrew in his report also stated that the churches progressed under the native Christians even with the absence of missionaries.[206] It is inspiring that these pioneers have laboured from the beginning of Kohima Mission Field as reported by J. E. Tanquist in 1926;

> The Kacha Nagas are asking the Mission to support a man in their midst ... The evangelists have all worked loyally, travelling and preaching the gospel. Every other month they have to come to Kohima to attend a Bible Class ... It was an inspiring meeting.[207]

Perhaps, as seen in the report, they have worked loyally even without the assistance of others, yet sometimes requests were made to help them. Then, they did not know how to tell of Christ effectively to others, but their simple faith and sacrificial efforts through itinerant preaching and communicating the word of God actively during the resistant period was the result of the growth of the churches today.

205 Dozo, *Hill Tribes Now for Tribes in India,* 21.

206 Elungkiebe Zeliang, comp., *History of Christianity in Manipur: Source Materials* (Guwahati: Christian Literature Centre, 2005), 53.

207 Ndang, *Zeme Baptist Church Council,* 2-3.

2. Methods of Local Evangelists: Exploring their Contributions and Footprints

2.1. Evangelistic Itineration

Unlike foreign missionaries who established schools and built hospitals as part of their ministry, Zeliang local evangelists reached out to the people with barefoot embedded with the basic word of God. Indeed, this method was the point of deviation from other missionary activities. Perhaps this was due to the lack of sponsorship and financial constraint. Nevertheless, fund constraint was never a discouraging factor, the enthusiastic endeavour of the native evangelists brought much fruits and together with them, the early converts collectively became pioneers among the people with the advantage of ethnic and cultural commonality.[208] The evangelists resorted more on direct approach by extensively engaging in itinerant preaching from village to village, teaching the story of the gospel with the message of love and forgiveness and organised local churches. This was the focal point of the method followed by the early evangelists. They proclaimed the messages and the stories of the Bible to the people as far as possible to every place they went. Whenever they enter a village on evangelism, pastor's house is their first shelter to rest and the village morung is their ample place to preach the gospel. In this the morung provided the best place for them which were simply appealing despite hostile reactions and sometimes even in the course of evangelism they experienced the miracles of God.[209]

The tumultuous journey of the pioneers through their visionary leadership resulted in sowing the seeds of transformation and as such the Zeme Christian remains obliged for their sacrifices. Notwithstanding any circumstances bearing natures' fury and stiff opposition from their fellow tribesman, they held on to the truth to impart the discerning knowledge of truth and evil. As such today

---

208 Interview with Hainsu Kauring, Church elder, New Tesen Baptist Church, 19 December 2016.

209 Interview with Irangcangbe Nza, Field Evangelist, ZBCC, 21 July 2016. He is also one of the pioneer evangelists in the Zeme area.

we see a tremendous and enormous development because of their selfless sacrificial contributions.[210]

2.2. Literature vis–à-vis Bible and Hymnal Translation: Towards Affirming One's Identity

Literature is an important tool to unite and bring a community together. Having realised the importance of literature at the dawn of Christianity, Zeme intellectuals and more specifically the pioneer evangelists began to explore every opportunity to come up with a vernacular Bible and hymns. The Zeme had neither hymn nor Bible of their own apart from the *Hymns of Kacha Naga*.[211] Consequently, laying the foundation, Lungalang initiated the translation of the gospel of Matthew into Zeme dialect in 1954 during his stay in Kohima and in 1957 it was published by the Bible Society of India.[212] According to Visor, the effective mission lies upon the biblical knowledge, therefore, translation of the Bible into one's own dialect is also one of the great missions.[213] But fund constraint was the main drawbacks, yet a ray of hope came in the year 1954 through the CBCAM who extended a helping hand towards establishing Mission Centre at Ndunglwa. As such in 1956 in order to cater the need of the believers to have their own vernacular Bible, Keneise and Kaisungbo were entrusted to translate the *Gospel* into Zeme and Liangmai respectively with remuneration of Rs. 30/- per month through CBCAM. However, this work was kept in abeyance for some months due to some havoc created by Naga insurgency group with the Indian army in 1956. Thus, due to this reason the translation work was delayed and it also created a communication gap between the Bible Society of India and Zeme Church. Despite this imbroglio, Keneise remained steadfast to his work and finally the translated St. *John* gospel could be released in

---

210 Interview with Rev. Deuhing Nsa, Former Evangelist, ZBCC, 25 October 2016. He is also one of the pioneer evangelists in the Zeme area.

211 This hymn was the first of its kind for the Zeme, translated by Gwizao Meru and Tanquist in 1918, as discussed in the Second Chapter.

212 Ndang, *Zeme Baptist Church Council*, 85.

213 V. H. Zeliang, *Zeliang Nagame Na Tinggwang Sam*, 13.

1961.[214] Further he also translated the gospel of *Matthew*,[215] and together with Heipei, Gieneu and others, he could come up with the 2nd edition of *Zeme Hymn Book* in 1962.[216] Literature ministry did not pause, it continued and through the concerted efforts of the pioneering evangelists and likeminded educated people, Zeme Churches could translate and publish their *New Testament* Bible in 1977. This was followed by another publication of small *Pastor's Handbook* prepared by Lungalang to be used by the pastors and evangelists in those days.[217] Thus, through their efforts in translation works it had enabled the linguist of Zeme people to even come up with *Vernacular Dictionary*. Today, dialectical barriers amongst the Zeme are greatly reduced and have brought the people together enabling them to coexist as one linguistic community. Hence, the boisterous adventures that the evangelists experienced came to a culmination with an eye opener for many of the Zeme people to endeavour and cherish the foundation laid by the pioneering evangelists.

2.3. Mission Centre: A Shift from Wretched to Serenity

Upon the completion of his course and on his return from Jorhat, Lungalang being the Field Director was relocated to the newly established Mission Centre at Ndunglwa with four full time workers. It is also pertinent to state that while he was in Ndunglwa, he along with Iteineung were engaged in teaching ministry leaving the task of translation works to Keneise and Kaisungbo.[218]

However, the dream and aspiration to construct permanent office in the new Mission Centre was cut short due to the conflict between the Naga and the India army. This imbroglio brought damages to a great extent to the association, infringed and burnt the timber work which was in progressed and even infested their

214 Pame, *History of Zeliangrong Baptist Church in Nagaland*, 66.

215 Changsang, "A Brief Life History of Naga Leaders in the 20th Century," 24.

216 Ndang, *Zeme Baptist Church Council*, 86.

217 *Zeliangrong Baptist Association Nagaland Silver*, 25.

218 E. Zeliang, "Rev. Heizieding Kediteiheing Lungalang Teilung Ha," 15 November 2016.

literature materials that they were working on. Thus in 1957, sensing the gravity of the situation, and after prolong deliberations and negotiations with the government and the land owners, the Mission Centre was shifted to Peren town in 1957. This development came at a time when the association was in its infant stage and was learning to crawl. Indeed, the period of 1953-1960 must have been some turbulent years for Lungalang and his colleagues in the association. In one of his reports he wrote, "Illiteracy with bad communications is the biggest barriers to the preaching of the gospel."[219] However, he stood tall against all odds, and galvanized his people to embrace Christ. As a matter of fact, Lungalang came to his people like Moses and led his people for 25 years as the Director of the association. In his leadership Zeme churches have experienced a rapid growth, and the mission centre was established in Peren Town in 1957. Today this mission centre is catering the needs of the churches in and around Peren District and beyond.

2.4. Educational Institutions: Towards Reformation of the Society

For any community to progress, education is the pillar and backbone of the society. The early field workers like Turi, Keneise were working tirelessly in all areas for their people. Slowly as the number of Christians increased, they began to understand the value of education that came along with Christianity. A positive changes and an advancement of life through education was felt. Thus, a new school was initiated to establish in Tesen at Tesangki in 1944 through the initiation of Turi to promote new meaning and understanding of Christian education. This school run and functioned under the recognition of Government until the Kuki and Zeliang separated to form their own association. Mr. Thangpau was the headmaster of that school with Intermediate Arts qualification. Deuhingbui, Seikholeit, Pauhei and Dihabou were the four teachers. However,

219 Lungalang, "Zeliang-Kuki Association," 46.

the school did not last long there, and later this school was shifted to Peren which was taken over by the government in 1946.[220]

The Zeliang evangelists, aftermath the separation of Kuki and Zeliang association in 1953, the evangelists realised the need of having one such educational institute. Therefore, together with their task of propagating the gospel, they took a boisterous mission to establish a school after the establishment of their mission centre at Peren in 1957. As such through the initiation of Lungalang, Baptist Mission School, Peren was established in 1964, with the vision to impart the knowledge of God through education. However, this was made possible through the contributions and efforts of many likeminded leaders who equally shared the burden of uplifting their people. Another Baptist English School, in Jalukie was established in 1970 with the vision to promote and propagate the Baptist faith and to produce competent leaders for the younger generations.[221] The magnanimous journey of establishing schools did not turn futile, in a short period of years the people began to reap the benefits. Indeed, it is said that when Lungalang retired in 1976, the schools that were established could able to provide teachers for twelve villages.[222] Apart from this achievement, the schools have also produced many intellects, bureaucrats, police officers and public figures, people of influence and public conscience. Even to this day the schools that were established by the pioneering and visionary evangelists stands in awe to testify their legacy.

3. Unveiling the Diary of Missionary Journeys

The Zeme History says that the Zeme church had experienced great years of stagnation during the period 1899 to 1925. During those days mass conversion was never the order of the day, accepting an individual in to the church and to perform baptism rite solely

220 Kaichamliu, *A Short Biography of Late Rev. Turi Kourinta. 1920-1993.* (Nagaland: Machiheing Ndang Printing Press, Peren, 2012), 2.

221 *Zeliangrong Baptist Association Nagaland*, 22-23.

222 E. Zeliang, "Rev. Heizieding Kediteiheing Lungalang Teilung Ha," 15 November 2016.

rest under the prerogative of the American Baptist Missionaries.[223] Therefore, till 1926 establishment of new church did not arise especially after the early death of Heizieluing in 1918, who served as the first evangelist.[224] His departure has created a void and the desire for having committed and competent evangelists was felt by the believers and in such a time Keneise came in to the picture to shoulder the responsibility of tending the sheep. In 1926, he was appointed as the first evangelist of the newly formed ZKA.[225] He shouldered the responsibility of propagating the gospel until Lungalang entered in to the arena of mission field to boost his enthusiasm. Lungalang knowing the status of the poor growth set himself immediately to work and shouldered every responsibility despite all difficulties and laid the foundation for the greater future prospects of his people. Especially when he was requested by Houston from KMF to tour around the Zeliang area for the mission, he began his itinerate ministry from village to village along with Keneise. Their first missionary journey as companion began in May 1951 and they landed in their native village. However, they encountered the hostile environment and were not even allowed to enter their village. The religious beliefs were too strong that it demanded every individual to adhere and observe gennas with utmost sincerity and reverence. As such because of this reason they slept outside the gate of the village until next the day and proceeded towards Ndunglwa, Mhai, Peren, Tesen, Tening, Tepun villages. To their amazement when they reached Tepun they found that there was a family who professed themselves as Christian but was in a desperate need of having a fellowship. In encountering them, they took them out of the village and were given water baptism by Kenesie. From there, they proceeded towards Ntu, Nzau, and reached Kendung where they found only one Christian family with only two households in the village after the Kuki shifted from their place. Then they moved to the next destination and reached Jalukie where they had fellowship with two Christian families, one was Zieluiheing family.

223 *Benreu Baptist Church Centenary,* 23.

224 *Benreu Baptist Church Centenary,* 24-25.

225 V. H. Zeliang, *Zeliang Nagame Na Tinggwang Sam*, 11.

Heningkunglwa, Kaibung, Mutbung, Khengzang and returned to Kohima.[226] Nevertheless, this journey was never the end, walking all through the rough terrains bearing the heats and brunt of nature, shedding tears in the midst of their journey, the hope of planting churches and propagating the gospels did not die down. Their mission depicts the missionary journey of Paul and the early church missionaries, travelling far and wide, sometimes together and many a time taking a lonely journey all for the sake of the gospel, especially in the case of Lungalang. Howard Houston remarked that;

> Lungalang was working in the area of rugged and lonesome covering all the area, being neglected for mission without any jeep road and only handful Christians of around 900 amongst many non-Christians who fully believe in their ancient worship.[227]

Ubiquitously, it is because of people like Keneise, Turi, Lungalang, Hazieding, Wisung Christianity had its preponderance in all the Zeliang villages in Nagaland.

4. Church Planting and Baptism

Besides the prominent works of Lungalang and Keneise, the Zeliang community were also blessed by the person of Wisungbo and Turi. Wisungbo possessed the gift of memorising Bible verses which he acquired at Bible class in Kohima, and through this gift he was able to strive and impart evangelism. He is also the founding father of the Tening Baptist Church established in 1926 specifically for the Liangmai speaking people. The church that he established was the third church, in the history of the Zeliang people which was made possible after undergoing several obstacles even to the extent of persecutions from the non-Christians. Yet today this church has become an epitome of his commitment and is presently the mission centre of the LBA today. Further he was successful in establishing

226 E. Zeliang, "Rev. Heizieding Kediteiheing Lungalang Teilung Ha," 15 November 2016.

227 Houston, *Nagaland Adventure*, 46.

Ntu Baptist church in 1928.[228] It is also very interesting to note that, before Ntu Baptist church was established, Wisungbo visited the village and warned the villagers in prophesy that he had seen horrid scene about the village. Accordingly, after he left the village, fire broke and burnt many houses which resulted in the conversion of many people accelerating its wave to other villages. Chewang remarked that Wisungbo was uniquely used by God that even to this day a person like him has not been born among the Liangmais.[229] The active work of Wisungbo spread to many villages as he evangelised the people which later resulted in the establishment of another three churches at Nzauna, Nkialwa in 1953 and at Lalong in 1960.[230] His work and sacrifice led not only to the conversion and establishment of the churches but also laid a great impact in the hearts of his people. Today the Liangmai of Tening village has established a hostel called 'Wisung Hostel' in his memory which serves the pursuing youths.

5. Miraculous Experiences: Excerpted from the Diary of Hazieding

Hazieding, like many of the early church apostles could perform so many miracles which people still treasures. Following are some of them:

a. On 9th September 1985 around 8:00 a.m. Hazieding and his team were at Ntangkam village on a missionary trip. A woman by the name Lungwangle was paralysed in the village and they were asked to pray for her. After prayer, the woman got a complete restoration from her ailment.
b. On 8th September 1986, Hazieding and his team Pauzie, Alungbe were at Mpai village on gospel tour. There was a young girl whose heart had stop beating and her eyes were closed. Miraculously as soon as they prayed and said Amen, the young girl gently opened her eyes and got well.
c. On 23rd July 1994 at Mbaupungwa village, there was a young woman by the name Ncuilung who was seriously

228 *Benreu Baptist Church Centenary,* 52.

229 Chewang, "Historical Study on the Impact of Christianity," 59.

230 *Tening Village Baptist Church Platinum,* 15.

sick and the people were in deep commotion. There Hazieding and his friends Hiaroiyi and Helang were in the village on gospel tour. When they visited her in the evening and prayed for her in Jesus name, the girl instantly got up, took bath and started serving them.

d. Another similar incident took place at Kendung village when a man by name Itingkiam was reportedly sick and requested them to pray for him. As soon as they finished praying the man got well and started singing the revival songs along with them.

e. At Tesen there was a young baby of about three months who was seriously ill and crying in her mother's lap. When Hazieding and his team laid their hands, and prayed, the young baby ceased crying and started smiling miraculously.[231]

f. At Hepunglwa, now Punglwa, Hazieding along with his wife and Heileuding were threatened with machete to kill and were accused them without reason but they were protected and saved. On the same day, fire broke out in Punglwa and gutted the whole village, but when Hazieding prayed to God 'Lord if it is your will that I should also be in trouble in time like this, let your will be done, but if it is your will to save me and my house from the fire, may your will be done, Amen', and miraculously, strong wind came blowing off the fire from the house of Hazieding, Heileuding and Heihaiyile, a widow from the opposite direction.

Besides all these miraculous experiences, he also had experienced a wave of revival that came to this people as early as 1958 in Hepunglwa village when Nsimlakpe had the first prophecy. This wave continues and became more vibrant in a booming manner towards the believers when Ms. Agwangle had prophesied again and Ms. Sineule had had her first vision during ZBCC revival in July 1977.

---

231 E. Zeliang, "Rev. Hazieding Teilung Ha," 15 November 2016.

6. Mission and Its Challenges: Towards Realising Its Goal

In the context of the hill tribes of the Nagas, persecution and opposition of the early Christians had been inevitable when the gospel was first presented. The early Christian period was not a smooth transitional period as much opposition was there from the majority non-Christian community. The early Christians had to make a bold decision to embrace the new faith to the gospel of Christ during the mission period because the non-Christians counted every conversion as a loss to the strength of their faith from the community. Thus, the early Christians had undergone severe oppositions and tough resistances from the non-Christians, yet the gospel did not die but prevailed.

F. S. Downs pointed out that most of the Zeliangrong villages strongly opposed Christianity and the Christians were invariably driven from their villages.[232] The early Christians often faced ill treatment and opposition from their own villagers. They have suffered both mild and wild persecutions. In most cases they were driven out from the community to new places. There were many instances of how the early Christians and the evangelists suffered trials from the non-Christians who were only their own fellows. Irangteing of Mpung village as discussed earlier, one of the earliest converts among the Zeme faced severe persecution and chased away from his own village.[233] Some were beaten, some were fined and some were imposed strict rules to follow the practices and customs of the traditional belief system. Thus, they were often accused and persecuted for violation of gennas. They were insulted publicly and punished to the extent of chasing away from villages and confiscated their properties. One of the prime reasons in the ancient villages that led to separation of villages was Christians facing persecution in their own homes and villages because of their new faith. They were banished and driven away from their community. The early Christians of Tesen village were driven away from their homes and this eventually leads to establishment of new Christian village

232 Downs, *The Mighty Works of God,* 124.

233 Interview with Nampiegongbe, M. Th Student, ETC Jorhat, 9 December 2016.

called New Tesen,[234] several other villages too had the same history of persecution and separation. Wisungbo from Tening village had faced similar persecutions and was despised by villagers. Hazieding was attempted to be killed several times by the non-Christians for preaching the gospel. He was even ill treated by his own clan to debar cultivation of any kind from their clan's land when he converted. Turi had to be arrested by the Indian army for preaching the good news. Likewise, evangelists like Keneise and Lungalang too faced similar fate at the hands of their fellow tribesman. Hence, due to this resistance movement, the growth of Christianity was gradual and was not progressive. And to add to their disappointments the movement of the violent Heraka movement of Rani Gaidinliu impervious to the gospel and the effects of Second World War had also dampened the spirit in one way. As such evangelistic efforts of the early converts, church activities and supervision of the churches were greatly affected. C. B. Firth said, "the Second World War, a part of which was actually fought in Manipur and Nagaland, adversely affected Christian work throughout the region."[235]

However, standing at the threshold of continuity and discontinuity, facing all sorts of problem and persecution, the spirit of the evangelists and the early converts did not dampen. Rather they were able to reinvigorate new methods in their mission reaching out to the people in far flung areas paving way for them to embrace Christ. Thus, Lungalang, in the report of 1967 testified that;

> Of all the years since I took over the works in 1951, May, this is the year for us with hundred new baptisms ... two very fruitful Bible classes were well attended, school is doing well and the leadership training is going on properly.[236]

---

234 Interview with Zugong Kauring, Deacon, New Tesen Baptist Church, 11 September 2016.

235 C. B. Firth, *An Introduction to Indian Church History* (Delhi: ISPCK, 1983), 266.

236 H. K. Lungalang, "Zeliang Baptist Association," in *Council of Baptist Churches in North East India: Eighteenth Annual Session, January 5-7 1967* (Assam, Nishangram: n.p. 1967), 73.

This report says that the work of evangelists did not go in vain but the seeds that they were sowing and have sowed were bearing fruits inspite of all the hurdles and oppositions. They have embarked on their arduous and strenuous mission during persecution from their own homes, witnessing the ill effects of wars, confronting various kinds of adamant responses from non-Christians.

Conclusion

The growth of the Zeme churches is attributed much to the lives of the early converts who worked tirelessly and sacrificed their lives in evangelising the churches during the early stage. Their works and contributions to the growth of Christianity and the formation of the churches through evangelism, educational concern, literature and church planting brought tremendous changes in the life of the people. Their lives which made a progress in Christianity were however followed by persecution and hostility, undergoing different miseries and sufferings for the sake of gospel. The church at the same time had undergone different stages of growth and decline during the formation period. However, it is to be realised that the established churches of Zeme today, the nature of their growth and the status of the Christian proportion is through the pursuance of the local indigenous evangelists who amidst their untold story of hardships and struggles have pioneered faithfully.

General Conclusion

The history of Zeliang people has been unique since the time of British administration as it generally covers the three states of North East India. Till today they are found in the three states of Assam, Manipur and Nagaland as they were being scattered to different administrative boundaries then. The indigenous community of Zeliang Naga who are predominantly found in Peren district of Nagaland are generated to modernity from the traditional society after their conversion to Christianity. The Zeliang society was brought into a better shape with the advent of Christianity with all its transformative factors besides the gospel of Christ.

The earliest Zeliang converts were students of Kohima Mission School which was established by the foreign missionaries to propagate their mission to the hill tribes of Kohima district. These first-generation Christians had come in to contact with the missionaries as early as 1897 and few of them were hastily trained from the mission station, whereas many were untrained. Nevertheless, through their conversion, the society began to evolve along with the steady growth of Christianity in the area. The growth of the Zeliang church and the Christian population was not progressive until 1925. However, as discussed earlier, with the help rendered by the native evangelists from the neighbouring tribes gradually the number increased. The assiduous works of the early converts in collaboration with the

Kuki Christians was also a morale booster for the Christians. Yet, this relationship was also cut short due to linguistic barriers with much hesitation. However, this separation has enabled the Zeliang to established their own mission enterprise and begin their own association in 1954, coincidently with the departure of Delano, the last foreign missionary in Naga Hills.

Thus, the context of Christian mission among the Zeliang was more or less an indigenous effort with the fact that even after the departure of foreign missionaries it did not affect the Zeliang churches because they were not depending on their aids. Yet, the churches were slow in its growth and experienced lack of leadership due to insufficient indigenous church leaders. However, even at that juncture, the pioneers of the Zeliang evangelists took up the task of evangelism colossally in the region of all the Zeliang inhabiting places. Therefore, it was a great period of evangelism by the pioneer local evangelists after the foreign missionaries, leading the churches to a great significant growth from 1960 onwards. The early evangelists were aware of the danger to tour around the non-Christians villages. Yet, their devotion and dedication to the Lord's command led them to work among the people and as a result converted many to new religion and established more churches. The history of Zeliang Christian mission may largely be attributed to local evangelists excelling more than the foreign missionaries in terms of speaking vernacular languages to their own people, adaptability to the climate and the conditions of the geographical environment, and the strength and potentiality in their peripatetic evangelism. They were the figures among pioneers who had demonstrated a calibre for their hard work. Their determination against all unusual experiences of mission, opposition and persecution for the sake of Gospel was commendable and magnanimous as far as the growth of the Zeliang church history is concern.

Tracing the history of these native evangelists, it is found that there are three major factors that have affected most to the growth of Christianity in the Zeliang area. One was the opposition from their fellow non-Christians who resisted with hostility and opposition. Another similar factor was the violent group of Heraka religion who confronted the evangelists with most hostile attitude and adversely reacted towards the progressive mission of the Christians. The third was the impact of Second World War which significantly brought the mission activities into halt. Despite, all these factors the local evangelists vigorously sacrificed in all possible means along with their wives. Besides, the revival movement as an agent of spiritual transformation also illumined the adverse factors and brought many changes in the life of the people. The experiences of the Holy Spirit and the obtaining of the charismatic gifts brought conducive changes to many nominal Christians and converted many non-Christians as well.

The sacrifices demonstrated by the early evangelists were commendable. They have forfeited their first choice of job and got out of their comfort zones for the cause of spreading the Gospel. The hardships and the oppositions faced by them in the course of evangelism were many and varied. Besides their contributions towards the growth of Christianity through evangelism and church planting, their literature and Christian educational concern towards reforming the society inevitably laid a foundation for the society to progress holistically. Schools were established in different places primarily to educate and promote gospel and to instil and promote the teachings of Christ. So also, publication of Bible, hymn books, and other basic church guide books had made a significant contribution towards the Zeliang churches. Overall their contributions have brought tremendous impacts in the society inaugurating a rechristened community which no sensible human would deny. Thus, however limited it may be, in spite of the limited recorded resources, attempt has been made to accurately present the factual works and contributions of the local evangelists of the Zeliang Christians towards it church growth.

Appendix

Photo 1:
Rev. Keneise Meru and his wife
(1903-1962)

Photo 2:
Rev. H. K. Lungalang and wife
(1919-2010)

Photo 3:
Rev. Hazieding Hairangbuing
(1922-1997)

Photo 4:
Evan. Wisungbo Nrak (Middle)
(1901-1977)

Bibliography

Books

A Brief Account of the Zeliangrong Nagas. Guwahati: All Zeliangrong Students' Union: AZSU, AMN, 2009.

A Peep into a Rich Naga Culture. Kohima: Directorate of Information and Public Relations, 1987.

Changsang, S, comp. *A Brief Life History of Naga Leaders in the 20th Century.* Kohima: The Directorate of Information and Public Relations, n.d.

Downs, F. S. *The Mighty Works of God: A Brief History of the Council of Baptist Churches in North East India.* 2nd ed. Guwahati: Christian Literature Centre, 2014.

Dozo, Phuveyi. *Hill Tribes Now for Tribes in India: A Challenge for Evangelization.* Calcutta: NMM: Nagaland Baptist Church Council, n.d.

________. *The Growth of Baptist Churches in Chakhesang Naga Tribe (India).* Kohima: Nagaland Missionary Movement, 1978.

Elu, Raitu., Haisoyi Ndang and N. H. Pouheu, comps. *Zeme Council North East India: Zeme Cultural Heritage & Customary Laws.* N.p.: Zeme Council North East India, 2012.

Firth, C. B. *An Introduction to Indian Church History*. Delhi: ISPCK, 1983.

Ghosh, B. B, ed. *Nagaland District Gazetteers: Mokokchung District.* Kohima: Government of Nagaland, 1979.

________. *History of Nagaland.* New Delhi: S. Chand & Company Ltd, 1982.

Howard, and Harriet Houston, *Nagaland Adventure, 1947-1953.* Dimapur: Published by L. M. Murry, 1987.

Hudson, T. C. *The Naga Tribes of Manipur.* Imphal: J. M. Printing Works, 1994.

"Irangteing." In *One New Humanity in Christ: Nagaland Baptist Church*

Council Celebrates Platinum Jubilee 1937-2012. Kohima: Documentation and Publication Committee, NBCC, 2012.

Kamei, Gangmumei. *The History of Zeliangrong Nagas: From Makhel to Rani Gaidinliu.* Delhi: Spectrum Publications, 2004.

________. *Jadonang: A Mystic Naga Rebel.* Imphal: 2009.

Keitzar, Renthy, ed. *Triumph of Faith in Nagaland.* Kohima: NBCC Office, 1987.

Kumar, B. B. *Naga Identity*. New Delhi: Concept Publishing Company, 2005.

Mills, J. P. *The Aos Nagas.* London: Oxford University Press, 1973.

Namthiurei, M. P. *The Great Awakening*. Manipur: Tamenglong GJ Publication, 1972.

Ndang, Suitei, comp. *Zeme Baptist Church Council (N): Pe Rehah, Petah nah Pemacet-Mariem, 1910-2000.* Peren: Published by compiler, 2002.

Newmai, Pautanzan. *The Basic Facts of Heraka Religion: Preceptress of Heraka Religion.* Imphal: Zeliangrong Heraka Association, NEI, 1993.

Newme, Ramkuiwangbe. *Tingwang Hingde.* Guwahati: Regional Zeliangrong Heraka Association, Assam, 1991.

Nsarangbe, Izieteilung. "The Belief in the Supreme Being from the Zeliangrong Nagas Perspective: Tribal Christian Theology." In *Tribal Christian Theology: Methods and Sources for Constructing a Relevant Theology for the Indigenous People of North East India.* Edited by Razosiele Lasetso and Yangkahao Vashum. Jorhat: ETC Coordination Program, 2007.

Nshoga, A. *Traditional Naga Village System and its Transformation.* Delhi: Anshah Publishing House, 2009.

Nuh, V. K. *50 Years of Peace Work by Nagaland Churches and Naga Civil Societies.* Dimapur: FNBA, 2014.

Pame, Rabi. *Culture and the Church: History of Zeme Naga Baptist Church NC Hills, Assam 1910-1995.* Nagaland: Nzauna Baptist Church, 2015.

________. *History of Zeliangrong Baptist Church in Nagaland 1897-1993.* Nagaland: Nzauna Baptist Church, 2015.

Pamei, Namthiubuiyang. *The Trail of Makuilongdi: The Continuing Saga of the Zeliangrong People.* Tamenglong: Gironta Charitable Foundation, 2001.

Pamei, Ramkhun. *The Zeliangrong Nagas: A Study of Tribal Christianity.* New Delhi: Uppal Publishing House, 1996.

Phillip, P. T. *The Growth of Baptist Churches in Nagaland.* Guwahati: Christian Literature Centre, 1972.

Puthenpurakal, Joseph. *Baptist Mission in Nagaland: A Historical Study and Ecumenical Perspectives.* Shillong: Vendrame Mission Institution, 1984.

Ramriwang. "Liangmai Baptist Association (LBA)." In *From Darkness to Light.* Edited by Alongla P. Aier. Kohima: NBCC, 1997.

Remei, Makulim. *Zeliangrong Union: The 71st Commemoration of Zeliangrong Solidarity Day.* Imphal: HopCom Offset Printers, 2005.

"Rev. H. K. Lungalang, Leaving Permanent Footprints." In *One New Humanity in Christ: Nagaland Baptist Church Council Celebrates Platinum Jubilee 1937-2012.* Kohima: Documentation and Publication Committee, NBCC, 2012.

Rivenburg, Narola, ed. *The Star of the Naga Hills.* Chicago: Judson Press, 1941.

Saha, N. "Ethnographic Study of the Zeliangrong Tribe of North East India." In *The Tribes of Northeast India.* Edited by Sabastian Karotemprel. Calcutta: Firma KLM Private Limited, 1984.

Sen, Sipra. *Tribes of Nagaland.* Delhi: Mittal Publications, 1987.

Shimray, R. R. *Origin and Culture of Nagas.* New Delhi: Samsok Publications, 1985.

Singh, K. S, ed. *People of India: Nagaland.* Vol. XXIV. Calcutta: Seagull Books, 1994.

Singh, Prakash. *India-The Land and People: Nagaland.* New Delhi: National Book Trust, 1972.

Singson. "Kuki Baptist Association, (KBA)." In *From Darkness to Light.* Edited by Alongla P. Aier. Kohima: NBCC, 1997.

Stacey, P. D. *Nagaland Nightmare.* New Delhi: Allied Publishers, 1968.

Suitei. "Zeme Baptist Church Council (ZBCC)." In *From Darkness to Light.* Edited by Alongla P. Aier. Kohima: NBCC, 1997.

Thou, Kangzangding. *Roots: A Collection of Zeliang Folktales.* Dimapur: Heritage Publishing House, 2008.

"Wisung: A Pioneering Pastor." In *One New Humanity in Christ: Nagaland Baptist Church Council celebrates Platinum Jubilee 1937-2012.* Kohima: Documentation and Publication Committee, NBCC, 2012.

Yeptomi, Najekhu. "Early History of the Nagas." In *From Darkness to Light.* Edited by Alongla P. Aier. Nagaland: NBCC, 1997.

Zeliang, Elungkiebe. *Charismatic Movements in the Baptist Churches in North East India: A Zeliangrong Perspective.* Delhi: ISCPK, 2014.

________, comp. *History of Christianity in Manipur: Source Materials.* Guwahati: Christian Literature Centre, 2005.

Zeliang, Visor H. *The Naga Baptist Family.* Kohima: Council of Naga Baptist Churches, 1988.

Interviews

Hengame, Paukwet. Deacon, New Tesen Baptist Church. Interview, 5 May 2016.

Kauring, Hainsu. Church elder, New Tesen Baptist Church. Interview, 19 December 2016.

Kauring, Zugong. Deacon, New Tesen Baptist Church. Interview, 11 September 2016.

Kedileuheing. Son of Rev. Hazieding, Ngwalwa village. Interview, 2 November 2016.

Lungalang, Epetlung. D. Th. student, UTC Bangalore. Interview, 20 November 2016.

Lungalang, Mteiziu. Son of Rev. H. K. Lungalang, Ngwalwa village. Interview, 27 October 2016.

Lungchi. Ex-pastor, Old Tesen Baptist Church. Interview, 21 September 2015.

Meru, Kulungsing. Son of Rev. Keneise Meru, Ngwalwa village. Interview, 20 October 2016.

Meyase, Leusi. Pastor, Ngwalwa Baptist Church. Interview, 20 October 2016.

Nampiegongbe. M. Th. Student, ETC Jorhat. Interview, 9 December 2016.

Newmai, Maithongphung. Pastor, Zeliangrong Baptist Church, Chumukedima. Interview, 27 August 2020.

Nrak, K. Lailu. Pastor, Tening Village Baptist Church. Interview, 24 January 2017.

Nsa, Deuhing. Former Evangelist, Peren Town. Interview, 25 October 2016.

Nza, Irangcangbe. Field Evangelist, ZBCC. Interview, 21 July 2016.

Putlang, Iriezeu. Ex-pastor, New Tesen Baptist Church. Interview, 12 October 2016.

Terieng, Izieteilung. Executive Secretary, ZBCC Peren. Interview, 20 February 2017.

Zeliang, Haireiwangbe. Evangelist, NC Hills. Interview, 11 October 2014.

Reports

Lungalang, H. K. "Zeliang Association." In *CBCNEI Sixteenth Annual Session, January 5-9.* Dimapur, Nagaland: n.p. 1966.

________. "Zeliang Baptist Association." In *Council of Baptist Churches in North East India: Eighteenth Annual Session, January 5-7 1967.* Nishangram, Assam: n.p. 1967.

__________. "Zeliang-Kuki Association-Naga Hills." In *Council of Baptist Churches in Assam, Second Session, December 29 1951-January 5 1952.* Nowgong, Assam: n.p. 1952.

_______. "Zeliangrong Baptist Christian Association Report 1967." In *CBCNEI Eighteenth Annual Session, January 3-7.* (Nishangram, Assam: n.p. 1968.

Tanquist, J. E. "Report of J. E. Tanquist." In *Assam Baptist Missionary Conference of the American Baptist Foreign Mission Society: Report Part II of the Thirteenth Session held in Golaghat, January 9-18, 1915.*

Souvenirs

Baptist Mission Church, Kohima Centenary Souvenir-1885-1985. Kohima: KMC, 1985.

Benreu Baptist Church Centenary (1997) Souvenir. Benreu: BBCC Committee, 1997.

Benreu Baptist Church Diamond Jubilee Reha 1981. Benreu: BBCDJ Committee, 1981.

Lungalang, H. K. *Kohima Field Baptist Centenary Jubilee Souvenir.* Dimapur: Ashoka Printing Press, 1985.

Liangmai Baptist Aruang Silver Jubilee Souvenir 2009. LBASJ Committee, 2009.

Mpung Baptist Church Diamond Jubilee Souvenir. Mpung: Souvenir Committee, 1988.

Poilwa Baptist Church Golden Jubilee 1938-1988 Souvenir. Poilwa: PBCGJ Souvenir Committee, 1988.

Tening Village Baptist Church Platinum Jubilee 1925-2000. Tening: TVPJ Committee, 2000.

Tesen Baptist Church Platinum Jubilee (2003) Souvenir. Tesen: TBCPJ Committee, 2003.

Tesen Baptist Nkwa Golden Jubilee Souvenir, 1928-1978. Tesen: TBNGJ Committee, 1978.

Zeliangrong Baptist Association Nagaland Silver Jubilee-1954-1979. Peren: ZBAN Silver Jubilee Souvenir Committee, 1979.

Sources in Native (Zeme) Language/Personal Correspondence

Kedileuheing. "Rev. Hazieding Bata Ha Rau Mdui Kega." Letter to the author, 4 November 2016.

Lungalang, Epetlung. "Apau Dade Raukelu Document on the Night of 25th December, 2008." Letter to the author, 28 October 2016.

Kaichamliu. *A Short Biography of Late Rev. Turi Kourinta. 1920-1993.* Nagaland: Machiheing Ndang Printing Press, Peren, 2012.

Zeliang, Elungkiebe. "Rev. Heizieding Kediteiheing Lungalang Teilung Ha, Personal Interview with Rev. H. K. Lungalang at his Residence at Ngwalwa village on 28 June, 1996." Letter to the author, 15 November 2016.

________. "Rev. Hazieding Teilung Ha, Personal Interview with Rev. Hazieding at his House at Heningkunglwa on 30 June, 1996." Letter to the author, 15 November 2016.

Zeliang, Visor H. *Zeliang Nagame Na Tinggwang Sam: The Zeliang Nagas and the Word of God.* Shillong: Rita Printers, 1982.

Unpublished Theses

Chewang, Alice. "Historical Study on the Impact of Christianity upon the Role and Status of Liangmai Women from 1925 till the Present Time." M.Th. Thesis, Eastern Theological College, 2013.

Haiku. "The Impact of Christian Gospel on the Traditional Superstitious Beliefs of the Zeliangrong Nagas." BD Thesis, Eastern Theological College, 1995.

Haisuitei. "A Historical Study of Christianity and Heraka (*Kampai*) Cult among Zeliangrong People in Nagaland." BD Thesis, United Theological College, 1989.